Ideas Matter

Considering Jesus Christ

John D. Gillespie

Myrrh Books

Overland Park, Kansas

Ideas Matter: Considering Jesus Christ
John D. Gillespie

Copyright ©2014 John D. Gillespie

Myrrh Books

Overland Park, Kansas

Library of Congress Control Number: 2014915953

ISBN: 978-1-940243-50-4

(Romans 8:1 All wrongs reversed)

Special thanks to Jim Kochenburger of ChristianWriterHelp.com and Nell Riechers for their help in preparing this manuscript.

Back cover photograph: Author at entrance to Auschwitz Concentration Camp, Poland.

*To my Tessa
With an eternally grateful heart
For our precious and uncommon union.*

TABLE OF CONTENTS

FOREWORD

We do not preach ourselves but Jesus Christ as Lord, and
ourselves as your servants, for Jesus' sake. For God, who
said, "Let light shine out of darkness," made his light shine
in our hearts to give us the light of the knowledge of the glory
of God in the face of Christ. (2 Corinthians 4:5-6)

You hold in your hands an inestimable treasure. You hold in your
hands the antidote to a superficial age. This book has the power to
transform the way you think about yourself, your life, the Church,
and the world. The reason this book can do that is its subject: Jesus.
The greatest need of every person today is a deeper acquaintance and
experience of Jesus of Nazareth. The greatest need of the world today
is for thousands of churches to be filled with people from all cultures
and backgrounds, ablaze with love for Jesus Christ. This book (and its
predecessor, *Beholding Jesus: Letters to My Children*) can fuel that
blaze in your heart and your church.

I have known John Gillespie for well over twenty years. It is my
privilege to be one of his friends. More than anyone I know, John has
beheld and loved the Lord Jesus Christ. He is just as passionate about
Jesus on the tee and at the table as he is in the pulpit and study. His
Christ-centred faith, friendship, and pastoral care have been a unique
encouragement to many people. Now, through this book, this encouragement can be yours as well.

I have given a copy of *Beholding Jesus* to all those who lead worship at the church I serve, and look forward to doing the same with this
volume. It is an excellent book for both personal and group studies,

and I have no doubt that it can be a significant book in your life. So, as John would say, "Go deep," and you will not be disappointed. "Go deep," and you will not be unchanged.

Chris Short
Pastor, Park Street Baptist Church
St. Albans, England

FROM MY HEART TO YOURS

Dear Friend,

My thesis is simple:

If indeed ideas matter, and they do, then ideas about the most important things matter the most.

It is impossible to overstate the need of the hour. Vertigo—ideological, moral, spiritual, intellectual, and relational—has our culture in a tailspin. Up is down and down is up. Right is wrong and wrong is right. Muddled thinking reigns in minds, homes, universities, governments, and cultures. In warring Muslim lands, wrong ideas about God are being sown, reaping their bitter and bloody fruits. In frivolous America, shallow thinking about God is leading to trivial living. In secular Europe the very concept of having ideas about God has long been killed, leaving the human spirit steel-cold and vacant. In the heaving Majority World millions of "gods" hold billions of minds in captivity to superstition and fear.

Ideas matter, and ideas about God matter the most. If you are familiar with my previous book, *Beholding Jesus: Letters to My Children*, you will know I am convinced that:

The most important thing about you is what you think about when you think about Jesus Christ.

That simple statement sums up my life, heart, and theology. But more, what a culture thinks about when it thinks about Jesus is the most important thing about it. Neither person nor culture can live above its ideas. None can rise above their view of God. Right living can only come from right thinking. That was true for Joseph Stalin, it is true about the East and the West today, and it is true about you and me.

Yet these are perfect days for Jesus Christ and His Gospel! He is the need of the hour, and is altogether able. This is not to over simplify or overstate. It is to understand. People and *peoples* need Jesus. We need to repent before Him. We need to tremble before Him. We need to run to Him. We need to trust Him. We need to fear Him. We need to cherish Him. We need to proclaim Him. We need to learn of Him. We need to rejoice in Him. We need to suffer for Him. We need to live for Him. We need to die for Him.

But first, we need to *think rightly about Him*.

There is no other hope for you.
There is no other hope for me.
There is no other hope for our world.

This book is a companion to my previous book *Beholding Jesus: Letters to My Children.* As with that book, I am sure that you will find more thorough, scholarly books about Jesus Christ. That won't offend me! Just remember, these letters are written from my heart to yours, with an aim to help us think biblically about Jesus Christ, to the end that we live valiantly for Him. I wish we could sit together, eye to eye, life to life, heart to heart, and help each other get serious about Jesus. As you read these letters, imagine that we *are* together, because that is how I have written them! I could use some time with you, and perhaps you with me! Let this book be that.

The Bible's Jesus (as opposed to the silly Jesuses we invent) is endlessly faceted, and therefore endlessly fascinating. He is mar-velous, inviting, shocking, surprising, frightening, comforting, con-fusing, satisfying, baffling, and altogether wonderful. He is Lord of history, Lord of eternity, and (phew!) the Saviour of sinners. He is the issue, the big issue. He is worthy of our clearest thinking. And only clear thinking will lead to meaningful living.

Be sure of this: Jesus Christ will not disappoint you. In most every other case it may be true that "familiarity breeds contempt." More often than not, most of us cannot last a thorough examination of every nook and cranny of our lives. Deep in his epic *Les Miserables,* Victor Hugo made just such an observation:

> Theodule was, we think we mentioned, the favorite of Aunt Gillenormand, who preferred him because she did not see him. Not seeing people permits us to imagine them with every perfection.

So it is with us. However, not so with Jesus Christ! Considering *Him* permits us to discover Him with every perfection! He will stand up to your scrutiny. He invites your investigation. He welcomes your exploration. The more beheld, the more considered, the more amazing and more wonderful He proves Himself to be.

Christians can (and do) differ on many things, but we had better come together and bow before our Lord Jesus. Our foolish and prideful talk is silenced before Him as all lesser issues take their humble place, and we are together awestruck. Jesus Christ is the only one who dares take centre stage in the individual life of the Christian, or the corporate life of His Church. The stakes are just too high to major on minors. We are in a battle for the very soul of this generation, and of those to come. We need to be definite and deadly earnest about both the need and the remedy.

As I write, the big news in little old Kansas is of a lesbian couple who, having engaged a male to sire "their" child, only to split up, are now suing the "sperm donor" for childcare money. (I dared not write "father," as that is a noble, meaningful, covenantal word). In another story, a local man is in the hospital, having suffered injury after he ran back into his burning house to rescue his...video games. We are a culture unmoored. The wild whirlwinds, spawned in a culture bereft on noble ideas, have blown us into what seems like another world.

"Toto, I've a feeling we're not in Kansas anymore," said Dorothy in *The Wizard of Oz*. I'm afraid you are, Dorothy, I'm afraid you are.

In one of Jesus' stories, it was while men slept that a bad man sowed bad seed into a good field (Matthew 13:24-30). The Church in our day has been tapping the snooze button for too long. We have been asleep when we should have been up and alert, snoring when we should have been watching, amusing ourselves when we should have been thinking, dreaming when we should have been picking fights with the powers of darkness.

The greatest thing you can do for yourself, for your family, for your neighborhood, for your culture, for your generation, for generations yet to come, for history, for eternity, is go deeper with Jesus. Going deeper with Jesus begins with thinking rightly about Jesus. Thinking rightly about Jesus begins with encountering Him in the pages of the Bible.

To this end I offer you these letters.

As before, I have included a hymn at the end of each letter. Written by those who thought well, and then ran well and finished the course, these treasures from our past can help us meet Jesus in new ways, so that we too may run well. Don't rush though them, for they will give up their riches to those who take time to dig deeply.

Below is a God and Gospel saturated hymn from a God and Gospel saturated man...a perfect beginning to this book. Following the untimely death of Jonathan Edwards, Samuel Davies became the second president of the College of New Jersey (later renamed Princeton University). While travelling through England, the young Davies was invited to preach before King George II. In the middle of Davies' sermon, the king was whispering something to his wife. Davies halted his message, and, addressing the king directly, said: "When the lion roars, the beasts of the forest all tremble; and when King Jesus speaks, the princes of the earth should keep silence."

May the Lion roar in our day!
Yours for the sake of truth in a desperate age,

John Gillespie
Overland Park, Kansas
August, 2014

****

Great God of Wonders!

Great God of wonders! All Thy ways
Are matchless, Godlike and divine;
But the fair glories of Thy grace
More Godlike and unrivaled shine,
More Godlike and unrivaled shine.

Who is a pardoning God like Thee?
Or who has grace so rich and free?
Or who has grace so rich and free?

Crimes of such horror to forgive,
Such guilty, daring worms to spare;
This is Thy grand prerogative,
And none shall in the honor share,
And none shall in the honor share

Angels and men, resign your claim
To pity, mercy, love and grace:
These glories crown Jehovah's Name
With an incomparable glaze
With an incomparable glaze.

In wonder lost, with trembling joy,
We take the pardon of our God:

Pardon for crimes of deepest dye,
A pardon bought with Jesus' blood,
A pardon bought with Jesus' blood.

O may this strange, this matchless grace,
This Godlike miracle of love,
Fill the whole earth with grateful praise,
And all th'angelic choirs above,
And all th'angelic choirs above.

Who is a pardoning God like Thee?
Or who has grace so rich and free?
Or who has grace so rich and free?

(Samuel Davies, 1723-1761)

*All our lives we might talk of Jesus, and yet we should
never come to an end of the sweet things that might
be said of Him.*
Frederick Faber

*Without doubt, the mightiest thought the mind can
entertain is the thought of God.*
A.W. Tozer

Letter 1

Consider Him Whose Love Is Immeasurable, Yet Knowable

*And I pray that you, being rooted and established in
love, may have power, together with all the Lord's holy
people, to grasp how wide and long and high and deep is the
love of Christ, and to know this love that surpasses
knowledge—that you may be filled to the measure
of all the fullness of God.*
(Ephesians 3:17-19)

Dear Friend,

The love of Christ is meant to be experienced. Certainly we need to theologically understand the "mechanics" of the Gospel as presented in the Bible. Because ideas matter, poor theology will help no one to experience the love of God. But both the Bible and the theology it gives us are intended to lead us to genuine experience. You can study a road map and see how to get to the Grand Canyon. You can read a travel guide about the Grand Canyon and grow in your knowledge and desire to see it. However, neither of these can replace the genuine experience of being there. True and right for what they are, their aim is to get you to and into the Grand Canyon. Those who wrote both map and guide would be disappointed if you were satisfied to the extent that you had no desire to actually experience the reality. Once at the Grand Canyon, smelling the air, beholding the vistas, descending into the vastness, you will be thankful for the map, for it got you there. You will be thankful for the travel guide, for it told the truth and whetted your appetite, but being there, you will be enthralled by the reality.

The Bible is the true, authoritative, sufficient, clear Word of God. Without it we cannot think rightly about God. What Archbishop Ramsay said to Elizabeth on her coronation day in 1953 is glorious and true:

> Our gracious Queen: to keep your Majesty ever mindful of the Gospel of God as the Rule for the whole life and government of Christian Princes, we present you with this Book, the most valuable thing that this world affords...Here is wisdom; this is the Royal Law; these are the lively Oracles of God.

The Bible is *the* absolutely faithful and true book about Jesus. It is enough, with the help of the Holy Spirit, to lead me to Jesus. However, in a sense, I am not satisfied with it, nor does God intend me to be. The Bible gives me more than itself. It gives me the real and only Jesus and *He* is the desperate need of my heart.

The *written* Word is to lead me to the *Living* Word. The hymn writer said it well:

> Beyond the sacred page I seek Thee, Lord;
> My spirit pants for Thee, O living Word!
> (Mary Lathbury)

Warning! Yes, of course, we seek the Lord Jesus in the Bible. That is why Christians have Bible studies, not séances. However, the Holy Spirit wills that we know Christ, not just about Christ. Many who love their Bibles have yet to move with their Bibles to Jesus Himself.

Look at the scripture passage at the top of this letter. These words are rich. They tell us that we are to *know* the love of Christ, which *surpasses* natural knowledge. We are to know the unknowable. This is the intended Christian experience. This is where the Bible wants to take us. We should not allow ourselves to be satisfied with less. We need to pound upon Heaven's door, earnestly asking the Lord to forbid that we be satisfied with anything less than experiencing the love which surpasses all knowledge. (It *will* open!)

The word, *know,* in this passage means *to be aware of, to feel, to perceive, to understand, to be sure.* Thus, it involves the intellect, vitally so, but it goes beyond the intellect to embrace the entire being. It is an experiential word. *Knowing* goes beyond the road map, and with guidebook in hand, begins the descent into the depths of the reality. The air changes. The light deepens. The senses heighten. The heart quickens. Everything is somehow more alive. Conversation focuses. Self reduces. Trivialities are forgotten. A sense of glory increases. You are in the process of knowing something unknowable from a distance. You are perceiving something otherwise imperceptible, feeling something inexplicable, becoming aware of things otherwise hidden.

This is the intent of the Holy Spirit in authoring the Bible. It is to bring us to the beginning of an experience of the love of Christ that will grow into eternity. God the Holy Spirit intends to give us the power to do the otherwise impossible: *grasp* the immeasurable nature of the love of Christ. The King James Version uses the word, *comprehend.* It means *to take eagerly, to seize, to possess, to apprehend.* Do you see what God wants? He wants to give you the supernatural ability to get a grip on what you never naturally could—the immensity of the love of God in Christ:

- Its *breadth*: God's love is as wide as the whole human race. It excludes no tribe, tongue, or nation.

- Its *length*: It is as long as history itself, for it existed before the world began, and will exist when this world is long gone.

- Its *height*: It flows from the very throne of Heaven.

- Its *depth*: It reaches to the lowest depths of sinful human existence.

God's aim for the simple Christian is nothing short of knowing the unknowable, and experiencing the immeasurable. This is not "deluxe" Christianity reserved for a select few; it is intended to be the experience of the ordinary believer. Unfortunately, many believers are satisfied with map and book, even as the magnificent reality beckons. Of course, the love of God cannot be experienced in *full* this side of Heaven. However, that does not mean it cannot be genuinely and increasingly experienced here and now. The problem is that we are satisfied too easily. We can even dog-ear our Bible, memorize it, and tote it everywhere, but not do what its Author wants us to do with it, namely, experience *Him.*

The apostle's prayer for the Ephesians applies to us as surely as to them. We dare not gloss over it. We dare not miss its impact. We dare not be satisfied until we begin to feel the indescribable, to the end that we are "filled to the measure of all the fullness of God" (Ephesians 3:19). I am not even sure what this means! However, it is more than what I have known until now.

Armed with the encouragement that God wants me to know the unknowable, this is what I am going to do (and I encourage you to do the same): I am going to open my Bible, put it on the floor, get on my knees before it, and *pound on Heaven's door*, asking my Heavenly Father to bring me into an ever deepening relationship with Jesus Christ. Then, as God takes me deeper into the experience of the love of Christ, by grace, it will be my aim to ask for more, and more, and more, so that my capacity for fullness might be ever increasing, to the end that I am being forever filled to the measure of the fullness of God.

I shall then be, in the words of Richard Baxter, "in the suburbs of Heaven."

****

Break Thou the Bread of Life

Break Thou the bread of life, dear Lord, to me,
As Thou didst break the loaves beside the sea;
Beyond the sacred page I seek Thee, Lord;
My spirit pants for Thee, O living Word!

Bless Thou the truth, dear Lord, to me, to me,
As Thou didst bless the bread by Galilee;
Then shall all bondage cease, all fetters fall;
And I shall find my peace, my all in all.

Thou art the bread of life, O Lord, to me,
Thy holy Word the truth that saveth me;
Give me to eat and live with Thee above;
Teach me to love Thy truth, for Thou art love.

O send Thy Spirit, Lord, now unto me,
That He may touch my eyes, and make me see:
Show me the truth concealed within Thy Word,
And in Thy Book revealed I see the Lord.

(Mary Lathbury, 1841-1913)

Letter 2

Consider Your Merciful High Priest

*For we do not have a high priest who is unable to empathize
with our weaknesses, but we have one who has been tempted
in every way, just as we are—yet he did not sin.*
(Hebrews 4:15)

Beloved,

Nothing will do you as much good as a bigger, clearer view of God—
who He is in His majesty, purity, and nature. Moses was a man gripped
by the greatness of God. He would not fit comfortably into most of our
churches. His great hymn of praise, Psalm 90, soars with a sense of
the greatness and holiness of God...It lifts the reverent reader beyond
the world of trivial thinking, leaving him at the same time humbled
and stirred:

> Lord, you have been our dwelling place throughout all
> generations.
>
> Before the mountains were born or you brought forth the whole
> world, from everlasting to everlasting you are God.
>
> You turn people back to dust, saying, "Return to dust, you
> mortals."
>
> A thousand years in your sight are like a day that has just gone
> by, or like a watch in the night.
>
> Yet you sweep people away in the sleep of death—they are
> like the new grass of the morning:

In the morning it springs up new, but by evening it is dry and withered.

We are consumed by your anger and terrified by your indignation.

You have set our iniquities before you, our secret sins in the light of your presence. All our days pass away under your wrath; we finish our years with a moan.

Our days may come to seventy years, or eighty, if our strength endures; yet the best of them are but trouble and sorrow, for they quickly pass, and we fly away.

If only we knew the power of your anger! Your wrath is as great as the fear that is your due.

Teach us to number our days, that we may gain a heart of wisdom.

Relent, Lord! How long will it be? Have compassion on your servants.

Satisfy us in the morning with your unfailing love, that we may sing for joy and be glad all our days.

Make us glad for as many days as you have afflicted us, for as many years as we have seen trouble.

May your deeds be shown to your servants, your splendor to their children.

May the favor of the Lord our God rest on us; establish the work of our hands for us—yes, establish the work of our hands.

Most of us entertain paltry notions of God. When we do think of Him, our thoughts are often unworthy of Him, as we manufacture a "god" basically like us, only bigger and marginally better.

John Calvin was right: Our minds and our hearts are idol factories. We speak glibly of "the man upstairs," and the "old man in the sky." We boast that, "When I get to Heaven, He is going to have to give me a few answers." We imagine ourselves barging into His presence, by right, on our own steam, and in our own name.

Brazen foolishness.

Our view of God is way off.

Psalm 15 begins with two questions of profound importance: "Lord, who may dwell in your sacred tent? Who may live on your holy mountain?" (Psalm 15:1).

Those are great questions! Who even thinks to ask such questions these days? There is a *reverence* to them. They recognize a *problem*... a *serious* problem: Who can stand in the presence of such holiness? The psalm then provides the answer:

> The one whose walk is blameless, who does what is righteous.
> (Psalm 15:2)

Well, that's it for me. I'm out. If there is one thing certain about me, it is that my walk is anything but blameless, and I have often done what is *un*righteous. Accordingly, on my own, I cannot approach God. He is holy and I am not—plain and simple. This needs to sink in. It needs to affect me. It needs to humble me. It needs to undo me. Otherwise, my view of God is *way* off.

The God of the Bible, the *real* God, is two things at the same time: 1) He is *transcendent*, which means, He is *wholly above and beyond us*—totally *other;* 2) He is *immanent*, which means, He is *nearer to us than we can ever imagine*—totally *here.* In this, Christianity is unique. The made-up god of Islam—Allah—is totally other, but not near; revered, yet unknowable. The gods of Hinduism are near, just like us (only a little bigger), knowable, but not worthy of our deepest reverence. (There are some Hindu/Sikh streams with speak of a grand, Almighty God, but not finally knowable in the Christian sense.)

God—the Bible's God—is so far beyond us, so utterly holy, so pure, that we can *never, ever* approach Him on our own, by ourselves. No way. However, in Jesus, He has come near—tremblingly near...

marvelously near...mercifully near...miraculously near. He is wholly other and wholly one with us.

Because God is both transcendent and immanent, He is both the *problem* and the *solution* at the same time. This holy, unapproachable God has provided a living way to approach Him, to know Him, to genuinely relate to Him.

I am going to introduce the word, *priest,* here. I almost hesitate to do so, because, while there are certainly many sincere and dedicated priests in the world, the word comes down to us with misconceptions and preconceptions (some deserved, some not). What comes to your mind when you hear the word, *priest*? A distant, aloof, religious professional? Forget the misconceptions, because I want to introduce you to the only Priest you will ever need, the one who makes even the best of the rest redundant.

In reference to Jesus Christ, the word, *Priest,* is beautiful:

Think of one who cleanses.

Think of a friend.

Think of an advocate.

Think of a bridge.

Think of a way back.

Think of a mediator.

Jesus, God with Us, Emmanuel, the Son of God, God the Son, the sin-bearing Saviour, is our Priest. Through bearing our sin upon Himself on the cross, He has opened a living way by which we can approach His Father. In His victorious resurrection and ascension, He lives forever to keep us secure before His Father. Consider the following:

For there is one God and one mediator between God and mankind, the man Christ Jesus. (1 Timothy 2:5)

Who then is the one who condemns? No one. Christ Jesus who died—more than that, who was raised to life— is at the right hand of God and is also interceding for us. (Romans 8:34)

Because Jesus lives forever, he has a permanent priesthood. Therefore he is able to save completely those who come to God through him, because he always lives to intercede for them. Such a high priest truly meets our need—one who is holy, blameless, pure, set apart from sinners, exalted above the heavens. Unlike the other high priests, he does not need to offer sacrifices day after day, first for his own sins, and then for the sins of the people. He sacrificed for their sins once for all when he offered himself. For the law appoints as high priests men in all their weakness; but the oath, which came after the law, appointed the Son, who has been made perfect forever. (Hebrews 7:24-28)

This is all about a *relationship* with God—impossible because of our sinfulness, but made secure because of Jesus:

Now this is eternal life: that they know you, the only true God, and Jesus Christ, whom you have sent. (John 17:3)

The blood of Jesus, shed once on Calvary's cross, is sufficient to cleanse us from sin *at depth*:

If we walk in the light, as he is in the light, we have fellowship with one another, and the blood of Jesus, his Son, purifies us from all sin. (1 John 1:7)

This blood, shed once, speaks a *continual* word of pardon for the believer. Hallelujah! Heaven is open...and stays open...for the believer! Even when the believer sins, and the precious Holy Spirit brings conviction of sin, there is a *real* way back, through repentance and confession, for the blood of Christ continually cleanses from sin:

> Let us then approach God's throne of grace with confidence, so that we may receive mercy and find grace to help us in our time of need. (Hebrews 4:16)

> Since we have a great priest over the house of God, let us draw near to God with a sincere heart and with the full assurance that faith brings, having our hearts sprinkled to cleanse us from a guilty conscience and having our bodies washed with pure water. (Hebrews 10:21-22)

Imagine! A sinner being able to approach the very throne of God, in his "time of need." What greater need can there ever be than of cleansing and pardon, and to find "grace to help"? Jesus Christ is the *only* true priest you will ever have, and the only one you will ever need.

We approach God the Father through God the Son, the friend of sinners:

> Jesus answered, "I am the way and the truth and the life. No one comes to the Father except through me." (John 14:6)

Here is a grand old Charles Wesley hymn. We need to once again learn to think such great thoughts about Jesus. Drink these words in and let them nourish your needy soul.

****

Arise, My Soul, Arise

Arise, my soul, arise; shake off thy guilty fears;
The bleeding sacrifice in my behalf appears:
Before the throne my surety stands,
My name is written on His hands.

He ever lives above, for me to intercede;
His all redeeming love, His precious blood, to plead:
His blood atoned for all our race,
And sprinkles now the throne of grace.

Five bleeding wounds He bears; received on Calvary;
They pour effectual prayers; they strongly plead for me:
"Forgive him, O forgive," they cry,
"Nor let that ransomed sinner die!"

The Father hears Him pray, His dear anointed One;
He cannot turn away, the presence of His Son;
His Spirit answers to the blood,
And tells me I am born of God.

My God is reconciled; His pardoning voice I hear;
He owns me for His child; I can no longer fear:
With confidence I now draw nigh,
And "Father, Abba, Father," cry.

(Charles Wesley, 1707-1788)

Letter 3

Consider Him Whose Kingdom Cannot Be Shaken

Therefore, since we are receiving a kingdom that cannot be shaken, let us be thankful, and so worship God acceptably with reverence and awe, for our "God is a consuming fire."
(Hebrews 12:28-29)

Dear Friend in Jesus,

Adolph Hitler boasted: "I will build the Third Reich, and it will last a thousand years!" It did not last a thousand weeks.

Proud Nebuchadnezzar proclaimed: "Is not this the great Babylon I have built as the royal residence, by my mighty power and for the glory of my majesty?" His kingdom became the haunt of jackals.

A century ago, Empress Victoria ruled over an empire upon which the sun never set. Today it comprises a rainy, debt-ridden island in the north Atlantic.

Historian Arnold Toynbe (1889-1975), author of the epic ten volume *A Study of History,* made this sobering, studied observation:

> Of the twenty-two civilizations that have appeared in history, nineteen of them collapsed when they reached the moral state the United States is in now.[1]

Sobering truth. We need to hear it. In such a shaky world, upon what can we build our lives? People used to say, "sound as the dollar" or "safe as houses," but neither means much these days. We need to make certain that we are citizens of an *unshakable* kingdom. Jesus Christ rules over just such a kingdom. Currently, it is not fully visible. We do not see it now in its complete array, but of this you can be absolutely certain: it is coming.

The wonder of this kingdom is nothing less than the King Himself—God: Father, Son, and Holy Spirit. It is He who makes the Kingdom of God invincible and unshakable.

> There is a river whose streams make glad the city of God, the holy place where the Most High dwells.
>
> God is within her, she will not fall; God will help her at break of day.
>
> Nations are in uproar, kingdoms fall; he lifts his voice, the earth melts. (Psalm 46:4-6)

God is not mocked. Kingdoms and nations that do not honour Him, He shakes. He has shaken scores—perhaps hundreds throughout history—for He *rules* history. Hebrews tells us that there is a catastrophic shaking on its way; one which will give the Richter scale a nervous breakdown:

> …now he has promised, "Once more I will shake not only the earth but also the heavens." The words "once more" indicate the removing of what can be shaken—that is, created things—so that what cannot be shaken may remain. (Hebrews 12:26-27)

When the dust of history settles—God having shaken out the nations as one would shake rubbish out of a bag—nothing will be left of all the once proud Reichs, kingdoms, empires, and nations:

> When the kings of the earth who committed adultery with her and shared her luxury see the smoke of her burning, they will

weep and mourn over her. Terrified at her torment, they will stand far off and cry: "Woe! Woe to you, great city, you mighty city of Babylon! In one hour your doom has come!" (Revelation 18:9-10)

...the kings of the earth belong to God. (Psalm 47:9)

At that time, one kingdom, and one kingdom *only* will be left. This kingdom, peopled by those once scorned, mocked, and marginalized, the blind, lame, and forgotten, and the old world's poor (the "poor in spirit," as Jesus called them):

- will be where Christ reigns in everlasting glory
- will have no end
- will know no more death, sickness, crying, or pain
- will be the home of righteousness

What is more, Jesus *wants* to give this kingdom to you:

"Do not be afraid, little flock, for your Father has been pleased to give you the kingdom." (Luke 12:32)

What a Saviour! Imagine a king who desires to share with his (unworthy) subjects his very kingdom! That kingdom is coming—a kingdom unspeakably glorious because it is the realm of Jesus, the King of Kings! *Today*, we can become subjects of this, the Kingdom of God, through the wonders of the Gospel. No wonder Jesus tells us that entrance into this kingdom is *worth everything*:

"Sell your possessions and give to the poor. Provide purses for yourselves that will not wear out, a treasure in heaven that will never fail, where no thief comes near and no moth destroys." (Luke 12:33)

"The kingdom of heaven is like treasure hidden in a field. When a man found it, he hid it again, and then in his joy went and sold all he had and bought that field." (Matthew 13:44)

The focus of this kingdom will be God: Father, Son, and Holy Spirit. The splendor of this kingdom will be nothing less than God Himself. It will not be a place of sensual pleasure (as our Muslim friends say). It will not be a state of extinguished desires (as our Buddhist friends believe). Nor will it be the Hindu state of liberation from the body and the mind. It is real, solid, and weighty—a place where redeemed cultures and peoples will live in the very presence of God…the *glory* of it being nothing less than God Himself, present and all-pervasive:

I did not see a temple in the city, because the Lord God Almighty and the Lamb are its temple. The city does not need the sun or the moon to shine on it, for the glory of God gives it light, and the Lamb is its lamp. The nations will walk by its light, and the kings of the earth will bring their splendor into it. On no day will its gates ever be shut, for there will be no night there. The glory and honor of the nations will be brought into it. Nothing impure will ever enter it, nor will anyone who does what is shameful or deceitful, but only those whose names are written in the Lamb's book of life. (Revelation 21:22-27)

Gates which need never close and the absence of night speak of the unshakable security of the Kingdom of God. Oh dear soul, put yourself firmly in the hands of the wondrous King! All that is about us shall be shaken. However, there is a king who rules over a kingdom of grace, truth, safety, and righteousness. The surety of this kingdom is nothing less than the King of Kings Himself: Jesus. He is none other than the one crucified for sinners, and He is risen and reigns today.

I am so glad that I know King Jesus. I am so thankful (words fail me) that He had mercy upon my sinful soul! I am unspeakably grateful for His blood, which cleanses me from sin.

I want to live for Jesus!

Here is a wonderful old-time hymn we used to sing in the little Methodist chapels all over Staffordshire. I think we are too "cool" to sing such hymns these days. (Though isn't "cool" just another word for "lukewarm"?) Dwell on the great words of this hymn.

****

Sing We the King Who is Coming to Reign

Sing we the King who is coming to reign,
Glory to Jesus, the Lamb that was slain;
Righteousness, peace then His empire shall bring,
Joy to the nations when Jesus is King.

Come let us sing: Praise to our King,
Jesus our King, Jesus our King!
This is our song, who to Jesus belong:
Glory to Jesus, to Jesus our King.

All men shall dwell in His marvelous light,
Races long severed His love shall unite,
Justice and truth from His scepter shall spring,
Wrong shall be ended when Jesus is King.

All shall be well in His kingdom of peace,
Freedom shall flourish and wisdom increase,
Foe shall be friend when His triumph we sing,
Sword shall be sickle when Jesus is King.

Knowledge and fear of the Lord then shall be
As the deep waters that cover the sea;
All things shall be in the splendor of spring
And all harmonious when Jesus is King.

Kingdom of Christ, for thy coming we pray,
Hasten, O Father, the dawn of the day
When this new song Thy creation shall sing,
Satan is vanquished and Jesus is King.

*Come let us sing: Praise to our King,
Jesus our King, Jesus our King!
This is our song, who to Jesus belong:
Glory to Jesus, to Jesus our King.*

(Charles S. Horne, 1865-1914)

Letter 4

Consider Him Who Cleanses the Heart

And since we have a great priest over the house of God, let us draw near to God with a sincere heart and with the full assurance that faith brings, having our hearts sprinkled to cleanse us from a guilty conscience and having our bodies washed with pure water. (Hebrews 10:21-22)

Dear Friend,

Henry Gerecke pastored perhaps the most remarkable church in history. He did not pastor this particular church for long—less than a year. His congregation was not at all large—eight at the most. However, this Missouri farm boy who grew to become a diligent Lutheran minister had one of the most remarkable ministries of all time—at least for a few months at the end of World War II.

Gerecke, fluent in German, was assigned to be the chaplain to the Nazi war criminals at the infamous Nuremberg Prison, in November, 1945. His congregation was made up of Hitler's men...men responsible for the deaths of millions of people: Hess, von Ribbentrop, Keitel, Doenitz, Raeder, von Schirach, Sauckel, Speer, Schacht, Funk, Fritzsche, Frick, Goering, von Neurath, and Rosenberg.

These were men of cunning and cruelty. They were not frenzied, but cool and calculating. Their names would all be found in the *Who's Who of Murderers,* if such a book existed. Their individual crimes were unspeakably horrific. Their collective crime was to lead an entire nation, continent—even the entire world—down a path to destruction. Along with Hitler, Himmler, and Goebbels, these men were the distilled essence of everything evil in the human race.

To such men—deemed beyond redemption by most—Henry Gerecke was assigned as a chaplain by the US Army, but even more so, assigned by God as an ambassador of Christ.[2]

Armed with nothing but the Gospel of Jesus Christ, Gerecke began to diligently visit each notorious prisoner. He spoke with them earnestly about the things of God.

On November 18, 1945, he held a Christian worship service for the most hated criminals on earth. Out of fifteen possible attendees, thirteen came. Week by week, these Gospel services continued. Pastoral visits continued to these men who were on trial for their lives.

Could Christ hold out any hope for such men?

(Does Christ hold out hope for you and me?)

Could God begin to break down such hardened hearts?

(Can God begin to break down your heart and mine?)

Slowly, secretly—sometimes imperceptibly—God began to do a work in the hearts of these men. Albert Speer (the minister of armaments), von Schirach (the leader of the Hitler Youth), Hans Fritzsche (a senior player in the Ministry of Propaganda) Sauckel, Raeder, Keitel, von Ribbentrop, and Schellenberg (the chapel organist, not on trial), all confessed Christ as their Saviour and only hope. Gerecke, ever careful with such matters, admitted these eight to the Communion table, kneeling with them to receive the Sacrament as they confessed their repentance from sin and faith in Jesus Christ.

Perhaps you are incredulous at this point, even protesting: "These guys were just trying to get off the hook with God and man!" Well, granted that none of us can see into the depths of a human soul, hear these words of Greneke, when he was asked that question:

I have had many years of experience as a prison chaplain and I do not believe I am easily deluded by phony reformations at the eleventh hour.[3]

Perhaps you have a hard time believing that Jesus Christ can or will forgive such horrible creatures as these. If that is the case, I am more worried about you at this point than about them, and I need to ask you a couple of point-blank questions:

1. Do you think yourself better than they?

2. Do you think that Christ's sacrifice was insufficient for such men?

In reply to the first question: We are no more righteous than they, and they are no more wicked than you or I. Before our holy God, we are *all* capable of no end of wickedness. Indeed: "The heart is deceitful above all things and beyond cure. Who can understand it?" (Jeremiah 17:9). The Christian doctrines of original sin and total depravity teach that we are all guilty, via the sin of Adam, and sin has infected every aspect of all of our lives. These war criminals simply were what we all are. Put in similar circumstances, there is no telling what you and I might do (or have done).

In reply to the second question: The atoning work of Christ on the cross was complete and is sufficient to pay for any and all sin. How? Jesus, as the eternal Son of God, being of *infinite worth,* was able to pay for the *all* sins of the elect by one sacrifice—Himself. This is not to make light of sin, but to magnify the power of the work of Christ on the cross, and the unspeakably glorious grace of God.

So far, all this is simply a preamble to the purpose and point of this letter: The phenomenal ability of Jesus Christ, via His death on the cross for sin, to cleanse sinners (us!) at the *heart level.* I present these war criminals as Exhibit A of what Jesus can do. I could have presented myself, but people mistakenly think I am a "good person," so I present these horrid men. While before God, they were no worse than you and I, their sin was so obvious, so festering, that they present for us the perfect test case for the Gospel.

These men were tried and found guilty of the following crimes: crimes against peace, planning a war, war crimes, and crimes against humanity.[4]

Of the eight who formed Gerecke's "church," Ribbentrop, Keitel, and Saukel were given death sentences. Don Stephens records the hanging of Ribbentrop, Hitler's foreign minister:

At 01.00 Ribbentrop was called for first. Before he walked to the gallows, he told Gerecke that he put all his trust in Christ. Ribbentrop was then marched to the first of three scaffolds. He climbed the thirteen steps to the trapdoor. The impassive soldiers and press representatives looked on. A guard tied his legs. An American officer asked for his last words. Ribbentrop responded: "I place all my confidence in the Lamb who made atonement for my sins. May God have mercy on my soul." Then he turned to Gerecke and said, "I'll see *you* again." The black hood was pulled over his face. The thirteen-coiled noose was put around his neck and he dropped through the trap door.[5]

Then came a surprise:

When it came to Frick's turn, Gerecke records that he received a surprise. Although Frick had been a regular at chapel services, and…had accepted a Bible, he never showed faith.... On the scaffold Frick, who never took communion, stood in front of the chaplain…and told him that secretly during the chapel services he had come to believe that Christ had washed away his sins. Then the door opened beneath his feet and he was gone.[6]

That such men could die at peace with God after these crimes does not make light of sin, rather it magnifies the saving power of Jesus Christ. Jesus does what no one and nothing else can. He cleanses right down to the conscience, to the heart level. You may never stand trial as these men did for horrible, obvious crimes. However, is there not some secret place in your heart where shame seeks to take up residence? Is there not some chapter you wish could be removed from the book of your life? Is there not some secret sin that you hope not a soul ever discovers? Cannot Satan, your adversary, your accuser, do a dance upon such secret, shameful areas of your life? Does not your heart and conscience need deep cleaning as surely as did Keitel's, Frick's, and Ribbentrop's?

Christ and His Gospel can cleanse the heart!

He did not discriminate between us and them, for he purified their hearts by faith. (Acts 15:9)

For the accuser of our brothers and sisters, who accuses them before our God day and night, has been hurled down. They triumphed over him by the blood of the Lamb (the atonement) and by the word of their testimony ("I believe in Jesus"). (Revelation 12:10-11, parenthesis added)

What, then, shall we say in response to these things? If God is for us, who can be against us? He who did not spare his own Son, but gave him up for us all—how will he not also, along with him, graciously give us all things? Who will bring any charge against those whom God has chosen? It is God who justifies [takes away sin and gives Christ's righteousness]. Who then is the one who condemns? No one. Christ Jesus who died—more than that, who was raised to life—is at the right hand of God and is also interceding for us. (Romans 8:31-34)

For my "light reading" (joke) I am reading through Martin Luther's, *A Commentary on St. Paul's Epistle to the Galatians.* I need to quote him here. How this mess of a man understood the wonders of the Gospel!

> Thus a faithful man by faith only in Christ, may raise up himself, and conceive of such sure and sound consolation, that he shall not need to fear the devil, sin, death, or any evils. And although the devil set upon him with all might and main, and go about with all the terrors of the world to oppress him, yet he conceiveth good hope even in the midst thereof, and thus he saith: Sir Devil, I fear not thy threatenings and terrors, for there is one whose name is Jesus Christ, in whom I believe; he hath abolished the law, condemned sin, vanquished death, and destroyed hell; and he is thy tormentor, O Satan, for he hath bound thee and holdeth thee captive, to the end that thou shouldest no more hurt me, or any that believeth in him. This faith the devil cannot overcome, but is overcome of it. 'For this (saith St. John) is the victory that overcometh the world, even our faith. Who is it that overcometh the world, but he which believeth that Jesus is the Son of God?' (I John v.4f)[7]

Friend, the *only* cure for the human heart is Jesus Christ and His wonderful Gospel. The blood He shed *once and for all* on a rough cross outside of Jerusalem is God's remedy for your sin and mine. The Gospel is what *God* has done for our vile hearts. Make much of Jesus to yourself and to your world! There is no other hope for the soul! There is no other medicine for the heart! There is no other cure for the conscience!

****

Jesus Paid it All

I hear the Savior say, "Thy strength indeed is small;
Child of weakness, watch and pray, Find in Me thine all in all."

Jesus paid it all, All to Him I owe;
Sin had left a crimson stain,
He washed it white as snow.

For nothing good have I Whereby Thy grace to claim,
I'll wash my garments white In the blood of Calv'ry's Lamb.

And now complete in Him My robe His righteousness,
Close sheltered 'neath His side I am divinely blest.

Lord, now indeed I find Thy power and Thine alone,
Can change the leper's spots And melt the heart of stone.

When from my dying bed My ransomed soul shall rise,
"Jesus died my soul to save," Shall rend the vaulted skies.

And when before the throne I stand in Him complete,
I'll lay my trophies down All down at Jesus' feet.

Jesus paid it all, All to Him I owe;
Sin had left a crimson stain,
He washed it white as snow.

(Elvina M. Hall, 1822–1889)

Letter 5

Consider Him Who Stirs the Heart

My heart is stirred by a noble theme as I recite
my verses for the king. (Psalm 45:1)

Fellow Follower,

What stirs your heart? Everything? Nothing? Beautiful things? Gruesome things? In our age, we are fascinated by the frivolous and overstimulated by the sickening. Most hearts have been so jostled and jolted by the endless parade of trivia that nothing of meaning stirs them anymore. Some, having been captivated by the grotesque and thrilled by things which ought to shock, can no longer find fascination with what is noble and pure.

Our hearts were made to love, engage, and feel, but sin's perverting power has dulled us to the beautiful and captivated us with the hideous. Yet our hearts *were made* to be enthralled by God:

One thing I ask from the Lord, this only do I seek: that I may dwell in the house of the Lord all the days of my life, to gaze on the beauty of the Lord and to seek him in his temple. (Psalm 27:4)

Psalm 45 is a prophetic psalm about Jesus Christ. Initially a wedding song for Davidic kings, there is clearly a much deeper, more glorious significance to it. The New Testament letter to the Hebrews tells us that this psalm is about Jesus by using it in reference to Him:

> Your throne, O God, will last for ever and ever; a scepter of justice will be the scepter of your kingdom.
>
> You love righteousness and hate wickedness; therefore God, your God, has set you above your companions by anointing you with the oil of joy. (Psalm 45:6-7, *c.f.* Hebrews 1:8-9)

The psalmist's heart was stirred as he considered the wonders of his king. When was the last time you considered the wonders of Jesus, to the end that your *heart was stirred*? A heart which *responds* to Jesus will only be yours as you *consider* Him. Do not be surprised at this. Your heart responds to anything that it thinks upon and considers. When you dwell upon your favourite sports team, or the person you love, or your children, thinking about their attributes, their ways, the unique things about them that you love, your heart becomes engaged by them and stirred towards them. So it is with your heart and the Lord Jesus. The problem is that we rarely consider Him. We rush by Him and move on to endless lesser loves and trivialities. This psalm invites us contemplate, speak of, and exalt in the Lord Jesus. The psalmist wants his words, his "tongue," to be as precise and inspired as those of "a skillful writer" (v.1). So, what follows in Psalm 45 are carefully written, stirring truths about our king, Jesus. Let's take time…time never wasted but well used…to *dwell upon Him* to the end that our hearts are stirred by, and our affections engaged towards, the most noble theme of all: Jesus Christ. By the way, if you want to exercise your mind and heart, have a go at Jonathan Edwards' "The Excellency of Christ." It will give you a workout, but do you the world of good! I dare you! [8]

The King Who Brings Good News to His Enemies

You are the most excellent of men and your lips have been anointed with grace, since God has blessed you forever. (v. 2)

Here is a king who is "the most excellent of men" (Psalm 45:2), "outstanding among ten thousand" (Song of Songs 5:10). Though holy, He welcomes us, though sinful. He comes with the Gospel, with grace, with reconciliation to those who have shaken a rebel's fist at God. Usually, kings kill their enemies! King Jesus comes to pardon, cleanse, and reconcile His enemies to Himself.

The King Who Battles for Truth

Gird your sword on your side, you mighty one; clothe yourself with splendor and majesty.

In your majesty ride forth victoriously in the cause of truth, humility and justice; let your right hand achieve awesome deeds.

Let your sharp arrows pierce the hearts of the king's enemies; let the nations fall beneath your feet. (vss. 3-5)

But this king, the sinner's friend, is a righteous king. He bears a sword, but with truth and humility. The Lamb is a Lion, and the Prince of Peace comes to kindle a fire on earth. As Jonathan Edwards says: "There is an admirable conjunction of diverse excellencies in Jesus Christ."[9] The day will come when the kings of this earth will call to the mountains and the rocks, "Fall on us and hide us from the face of him who sits on the throne and from the wrath of the Lamb! For the great day of their wrath has come, and who can withstand it?" (Revelation 6:16-17).

Some Jesus.

The King Who Reigns in Righteousness

Your throne, O God, will last for ever and ever; a scepter of justice will be the scepter of your kingdom.

You love righteousness and hate wickedness. (vss. 6,7)

Here is a king with nothing to hide: no closet, no skeletons, no secret affairs. His throne, now established in the hearts of untold millions, one day to be displayed in fullness, will last forever. Long after the heroes and princes of this present age have faded into the mist of time, King Jesus shall reign in unchallenged righteousness. Millions from every tribe, tongue, and nation, once wicked in their sin, are now redeemed and righteous by His blood, and shall live and reign forever with Him.

The King Who Reigns in Joy Over All

God the Father has poured joy out upon His Son:

Therefore God, your God, has set you above your companions by anointing you with the oil of joy. (v. 7)

However, there is more. It just keeps getting more glorious! Jesus is not an austere, somber king. He is not "religious"! His Father has poured His joy out upon Him. Jesus is joyful! "Above His companions"—that is, more than anyone, anywhere, anytime—this "man of sorrows, though acquainted with (our) grief" (Isaiah 53:3, parenthesis added), is within Himself and in fellowship with the Father and the Spirit, eternally and deeply joyful. *And* He shares *His* joy with *His* people. He wills that His joy may be in us and that our joy may be complete (*c.f.* John 15:11).

The King Who Is a Splendid Bridegroom

All your robes are fragrant with myrrh and aloes and cassia; from palaces adorned with ivory the music of the strings makes you glad. (v. 8)

You will *never* behold anything or anyone as captivating as Jesus Christ. You were *made* for this. He is dressed in splendour because He is splendid. He is made "glad" by the event of His wedding, and He is thrilled by His Bride (the Church). (Stop and consider for a moment, a glad, thrilled, holy, righteous God!) God's book begins with a wedding (Genesis 3:21ff), ends with a wedding (Revelation 21:2), and here in the middle, is a love song about a wedding.

The King Who Loves His Bride

At your right hand is the royal bride in gold of Ophir.

Listen, daughter, and pay careful attention: Forget your people and your father's house.

Let the king be enthralled by your beauty; honor him, for he is your lord. (vss. 9-11)

Here is a king who has a bride. He is a *lover*, and by the time we get to the end of the Bible, we discover that *we* are the object of His love, *we* are His bride. Somehow, this needs to take our breath away. (How can it not?) The Bible is a love song featuring Jesus Christ and His Church. Unlike some earthly husbands, He is *enthralled* by the beauty of His bride (whom He Himself has made beautiful— including *us!*) Unlike some earthly brides, she *honours* her husband, who is her Lord.

The King Who Receives the Tribute of the Nations

Daughters of kings are among your honored women; The city of Tyre will come with a gift, people of wealth will seek your favor.

This humble, righteous, just, splendid, warring, loving king will one day receive the praise and adoration of the "great" people of this world. Hence, the Father says to the Son:

Ask me, and I will make the nations your inheritance, the ends of the earth your possession.

You will break them with a rod of iron; you will dash them to pieces like pottery.

Therefore, you kings, be wise; be warned, you rulers of the earth.

Serve the Lord with fear and celebrate his rule with trembling.

Kiss his son, or he will be angry and your way will lead to your destruction, for his wrath can flare up in a moment.

Blessed are all who take refuge in him. (Psalm 2:8-12)

The King Who Glorifies His Bride

All glorious is the princess within her chamber; her gown is interwoven with gold.

In embroidered garments she is led to the king; her virgin companions follow her-those brought to be with her.

Led in with joy and gladness, they enter the palace of the king. (vss. 13-15)

What a picture of our salvation! He is the King, our Bridegroom. We are His bride, made glorious by Him who takes pleasure in His people, and beautifies the meek with salvation (*c.f.* Psalm 149:4, KJV). Joy, celebration, security, wealth, purity, thumping hearts—these are the realities of our salvation, here pictured in a wedding between the King and His Bride, the object of His love.

The King Who Reigns Forever

Your sons will take the place of your fathers; you will make them princes throughout the land.

I will perpetuate your memory through all generations; therefore the nations will praise you for ever and ever. (vss. 16-17)

He makes His sons princes. He lifts up the broken "that he may set him with princes, even with the princes of his people" (Psalm 113:8, KJV). So His fame is spread throughout the land and the generation; famous for who He is and what he does. Therefore:

The city does not need the sun or the moon to shine on it, for the glory of God gives it light, and the Lamb is its lamp. The nations will walk by its light, and the kings of the earth will bring their splendor into it. (Revelation 21:23-24)

Words fail me. How can we *fully* describe Jesus? The Scriptures are written that we may at least *begin* to know, marvel, and be stirred by Jesus. Psalm 45 is given by the Holy Spirit that we might consider and behold Jesus.

Here is something to chew on: Mission happens…it cannot *help but happen*…when our hearts are stirred in consideration of Jesus. The key to missions is not talking about missions, but about Jesus. When Jesus is magnified, the spreading of His fame (missions!) becomes happily inevitable. The world needs Jesus! May His Church be stirred by and to Him, to the end that "the nations will praise Him forever and ever."

****

Hail, Thou Once Despised Jesus!

Hail, Thou once despised Jesus! Hail, Thou Galilean King!
Thou didst suffer to release us; Thou didst free salvation bring.
Hail, Thou universal Savior, Who hast borne our sin and shame,
By whose merits we find favor! Life is given through Thy name.

Paschal Lamb, by God appointed, All our sins on Thee were laid;
By almighty love anointed, Thou hast full atonement made.
Every sin may be forgiven Through the virtue of Thy blood;
Open is the gate of heaven, Peace is made 'twixt man and God.

Jesus, hail, enthroned in glory, There forever to abide!
All the heavenly host adore Thee, Seated at Thy Father's side.
There for sinners Thou art pleading, There Thou dost our place prepare,
Ever for us interceding Till in glory we appear.

Worship, honor, power, and blessing Thou art worthy to receive;
Loudest praises, without ceasing, Meet it is for us to give.
Help, ye bright angelic spirits, Bring your sweetest, noblest lays;
Help to sing our Savior's merits, Help to chant Immanuel's praise.

(John Bakewell, 1721-1819)

Letter 6

Consider Him Who Invites
the Weary to Himself

*Come to me, all you who are weary and burdened, and I will
give you rest. Take my yoke upon you and learn from me, for
I am gentle and humble in heart, and you will find rest for
your souls. For my yoke is easy and my burden is light.*
(Matthew 11:28-30)

Dear Fellow Follower,

Imagine a God who invites the weary and burdened to Himself! Where
else but in the Bible do we encounter such a wondrous God? In religion after religion, the "gods" exhaust the "worshipper." It is really
important that you see this, because it is yet another way that following Jesus is totally different from "being religious."

Endless rituals and tiresome duties, heavy burdens impossible to
bear—all are incapable of bringing anything but despair and weari-
ness to the "faithful." In fact, more often than not, the more faithful
one is, the more weary one becomes!

It may be a zealous Muslim cutting himself to expiate his sins, or
a Hindu holy man rolling endlessly down a filthy street to extinguish
bad karma, or Buddha himself eating his own excrement in an effort (I
guess) to liberate himself from all desire, or the good Baptist/Methodist/
Evangelical never missing a meeting in the hope of proving his salvation.
Whatever form it takes, religion without grace is a wearisome burden.

Behold Jesus! Here is God, in human form. He is not burdening
us *with* religion; He is delivering us *from* religion. The background to

this great invitation is the rigorous religion of the Pharisees. Devout Jews were laboring under the heavy yoke of a stale, cruel Judaism. Our Jesus would have nothing of it:

> Then Jesus said to the crowds and to his disciples: "The teachers of the law and the Pharisees sit in Moses' seat. So you must be careful to do everything they tell you. But do not do what they do, for they do not practice what they preach. They tie up heavy, cumbersome loads and put them on other people's shoulders, but they themselves are not willing to lift a finger to move them. (Matthew 23:1-4)

> Woe to you, teachers of the law and Pharisees, you hypocrites! You shut the door of the kingdom of heaven in people's faces. You yourselves do not enter, nor will you let those enter who are trying to. (Matthew 23:13)

> Woe to you, teachers of the law and Pharisees, you hypocrites! You travel over land and sea to win a single convert, and when you have succeeded, you make them twice as much a child of hell as you are. (Matthew 23:15)

However, the God of the Bible, far from exhausting people, "gives strength to the weary" (Isaiah 40:29). He does not ask us to get all fixed up before we can come to Him. He does not expect us to reach some level of goodness first, because He is not the "good person's God," but the "bad person's God." Jesus Christ stands with arms open for you and me to *come to Him* as we are.

His invitation in Matthew 11:28-30 is unspeakably wonderful. It goes right over the heads of the arrogant and self-righteous, but finds a sure home in the hearts of the needy:

- *Come...all.* Here is an invitation as wide as the human race and as long as history itself. Do you see yourself in this invitation? Come to Him!

- *Come...to me.* Jesus is not subcontracting this all-important ministry to some archangel, prophet, or priest. He Himself wants to be our peace, our rest, our restoration. Look to Him!

- *All...who are weary.* Weary is what we do to ourselves—wearing ourselves out with no end of religion, striving, and sinning (is anything as wearisome as sinning?).

- *All...who are...burdened.* Burdened is what others place upon us—their expectations, their plans, and their agenda (and how heavy these can be!).

A wonderful invitation is matched by a sure promise:

- *I will give you rest.* How? Only one way: through the Gospel. He takes away the burden of trying to perform our way to favour with God. He delivers us from the impossibility of living in the vain hope that pleasing ourselves or others will give us peace. The rest Jesus gives is the rest of the finished atonement: peace with God.

- *Take my yoke upon you.* Drop that heavy yoke—the slave's yoke—and take the yoke Jesus gives! This is not a yoke given by graceless religion and graceless people, but the yoke of Christ, the sinners' friend: the simple yoke of simply trusting.

- *Learn from me.* The yoke is not just a burden-bearing tool, but a training instrument, under which the novice animal is placed in tandem with the experienced. Lo and behold, when you put on this yoke—Jesus' yoke—you look to your side, and there is Jesus Himself, under the other half of the yoke (the heavier half!). With a gentle voice, He says, "Now we are in this together...learn from me what it means to be a child of the Father."

- *I am gentle and humble in heart.* Jesus is not a slave driver, but a brother. He made us and knows our weaknesses. He is not behind us with a whip, but next to us, under the very same yoke. He patiently bears with us to the end, that we can go where we could never have gone if alone, or if yoked to another instead of Him. Some of us have been bearing a different yoke far too long!

- *You will find rest for your souls.* How our souls need rest! Rest is found when we lay down the heavy yoke of performance and take up the yoke of grace. Just receive this; see the word picture Jesus Himself is giving to you here. *Look at it.* Yoked to Christ. Learning of Him. Your soul finally at rest. Take a deep, deep breath, and let out a sigh of true relief!

- *For my yoke is easy and my burden light.* Satan is a hard task-master! He comes to ruin all that he can. Not Jesus. To those wearied by sin, Satan, and self, Jesus says, "Try my yoke: Is it not easy, and is not my burden light?" Through the forgiveness of sin, we are reconciled forever to our God, and the yoke we bear fits gently atop a robe of righteousness.

This glorious invitation was lost on the proud and arrogant, but not on the poor, the blind, the lame, the tax collector, and the prostitute. It is lost on many today. May it not be lost on you! Receive it as yours. It is a Gospel invitation…and Gospel invitations never grow old. They are ever new. You might be a believer in Jesus now for days or decades, still, the wonders of the *rest* given through the Gospel should only be deepening, never diminishing.

How I love the ancient hymn below by the Scottish pastor, Horatio Bonar. Let these words minister to you the deep, deep truths of Jesus, our incomparable Jesus.

****

I Heard the Voice of Jesus Say

I heard the voice of Jesus say, "Come unto Me and rest;
Lay down, thou weary one, lay down Thy head upon My breast."
I came to Jesus as I was, Weary and worn and sad;
I found in Him a resting place, And He has made me glad.

I heard the voice of Jesus say, "Behold, I freely give
The living water; thirsty one, Stoop down, and drink, and live."
I came to Jesus, and I drank Of that life-giving stream;
My thirst was quenched, my soul revived,
And now I live in Him.

I heard the voice of Jesus say, "I am this dark world's Light;
Look unto Me, thy morn shall rise, And all thy day be bright."
I looked to Jesus, and I found In Him my Star, my Sun;
And in that light of life I'll walk, Till trav'ling days are done.

I heard the voice of Jesus say, "My Father's house above
Has many mansions; I've a place Prepared for you in love."
I trust in Jesus—in that house, According to His word,
Redeemed by grace, my soul shall live Forever with the Lord.

(Horatio Bonar, 1808-1889)

Letter 7

Consider the Lord of Salvation

You do not believe because you are not my sheep.
(John 10:26)

Dear One,

Jesus can be tough—incredibly tough. Yes, it is written of Him: "A bruised reed he will not break, and a smoldering wick he will not snuff out" (Matthew 12:20). But this patient and gentle Saviour is not one to be taken lightly.

The Pharisees thought they had Jesus sorted out. "*We* are not going to believe in *Him*," was their proud conclusion. Confident of *their* sovereignty in regard to Jesus, they figured that what they "did" with Jesus was their call.

Jesus turned the tables on them. His claim is profound in its implications. Just consider what He says to the "big shots" of His day:

"You do not believe because you are not my sheep" (John 10:26).

Can you imagine the shock of those who heard that statement? Do you get the unnerving twist? Can you see Jesus pulling the rug out from under the proud feet of the Pharisees? Do you yourself feel a tug at the rug? You should. The one speaking here is none other than the very Lord of Salvation, the one who holds our days in His hands, who Himself possesses the keys of death and Hades (Revelation 1:18). He is the friend of sinners, but He dares not to be regarded lightly.

Thinking we are the centre of the universe and the captains of our destiny, we imagine a scheme in which Jesus is passive (helpless?) in regard to our salvation, and we are comparatively active and in charge of the matter. We think up a Jesus who tiptoes quietly amidst the margins of our lives, lest He disturb us in our busy agenda. We imagine a wilting, waiting Jesus, not a strong, aggressive Saviour. Therefore, we *expect* to hear Jesus say, perhaps with a sniffle and a tear:

"You are not my sheep because you decided not to believe."

In other words, we expect to hear Jesus say to the Pharisees: "*You* have not chosen *me*, (Oh! How I wish you had!). That is why you are not my sheep." This would fit nicely into our way of thinking, keeping us in control, nicely in charge of all things, including our destinies. However, Jesus says no such thing to the proud Pharisees. His statement, "You do not believe because you are not my sheep" (John 10:26) is a total put-down to these proud religious fellows. In effect, He is saying, "You are not a part of my flock because I have not chosen you to be so."

Now I can hear some saying:

"How unfair!"
"Those poor Pharisees!"
"How dare Jesus not choose them!"

I counsel caution here. Before any of us feel we can occupy some sort of moral high ground over Jesus in this matter, we will do well to consider the truths below.

1. Jesus does not *owe* anyone salvation. He is under no obligation to save any of us. His grace is free, unmerited, unhindered, and not compelled by anything good in us (Ephesians 2:8-9).

2. Nevertheless, Jesus never will reject one humble, broken sinner who comes to Him confessing nothing but need and faith in Him (Matthew 11:28; John 6:37).

3. Jesus is more holy *and* more merciful than any of us can or ever will be. His love is so much deeper, His righteousness so much purer than we can ever imagine (Revelation 1:12-18).

4. Jesus wills a populated Heaven, and aims to save sinners. He wants this more than we do. He came for the sin-sick, hopeless, and helpless (Luke 19:10).

5. Self-righteous religious people make Jesus angry. He does save some of them, in acts of incredible grace and mercy, but vast numbers of them perish eternally (1 Timothy 1:15; Luke 20:46-47).

6. Our loving and merciful Lord Jesus is not afraid to send deserving sinners to Hell (Matthew 23:33).

I cannot pretend that I understand the mystery and miracle of the sovereignty of God in matters of salvation. It is better to tremble and worship than it is to argue and pontificate. In the Gospels, the place where we authentically meet Jesus, He embraces and rebuffs, He welcomes and refuses.

We see a most gentle and patient Saviour…towards the contrite and broken. However, as it concerns the proud and religious, we do not find "gentle Jesus, meek and mild." We see a Sovereign Lord who rejects the self-righteous in their pride and promises them a certain Hell. The Bible makes it plain:

God opposes the proud, But shows favor to the humble.
(1 Peter 5:5)

We read and recite Bible verses like this one without allowing them to impact our lives. Do you see what God is saying here? The God of the Universe, the Lord of History, the one who determines our eternal destinies, who gives us our very breath, *stands in opposition* to us when we are self-centred, and self-righteous.

Oh dear.

If you need proof, read Jesus' warnings to the religious ones of His day in Matthew 23. You will see what I mean. However, make sure you read it on your knees. Keep a box of tissues nearby as you pray earnestly for a broken and contrite heart, and plead for grace to be found in your otherwise unworthy heart. Pray for the grace needed to see yourself in those verses.

Edward Perronet was a companion of the Wesleys. A reluctant preacher, he was nonetheless a man captivated by the majesty of Jesus Christ. Let this worshipful hymn enlarge your view of our awesome, majestic Saviour.

****

All Hail the Power of Jesus' Name!

All hail the power of Jesus' name!
Let angels prostrate fall;
bring forth the royal diadem,
and crown him Lord of all.
Bring forth the royal diadem,
and crown him Lord of all.

Ye chosen seed of Israel's race,
ye ransomed from the fall,
hail him who saves you by his grace,
and crown him Lord of all.
Hail him who saves you by his grace,
and crown him Lord of all.

Sinners, whose love can ne'er forget
the wormwood and the gall,
go spread your trophies at his feet,
and crown him Lord of all.
Go spread your trophies at his feet,
and crown him Lord of all.

Let every kindred, every tribe
on this terrestrial ball,
to him all majesty ascribe,
and crown him Lord of all.
To him all majesty ascribe,
and crown him Lord of all.

Crown him, ye martyrs of your God,
who from his altar call;
extol the Stem of Jesse's Rod,
and crown him Lord of all.
Extol the Stem of Jesse's Rod,
and crown him Lord of all.

O that with yonder sacred throng
we at his feet may fall!
We'll join the everlasting song,
and crown him Lord of all.
We'll join the everlasting song,
and crown him Lord of all.

(Edward Perronet, 1726-1792;
Final verse by John Rippon, 1787)

Letter 8

Consider Him Who Will Terrify the Wicked

Then the kings of the earth, the princes, the generals, the
rich, the mighty, and everyone else, both slave and free, hid
in caves and among the rocks of the mountains. They called
to the mountains and the rocks, "Fall on us and hide us from
the face of him who sits on the throne and from the wrath of
the Lamb! For the great day of their wrath has come, and
who can withstand it?"
(Revelation 6:15-17)

Dear Fellow Beholder,

The world we live in thinks it is finished with Jesus. It has yet to start with Him. The Bible teaches that history is moving towards a fixed day. On God's calendar, if you will, there is a day with a red "X" marked on it. The day will come when Jesus Christ will return; this time not as a baby to be swaddled, but as a king with whom to reckon.

People laugh at this. Endless efforts are being made to reduce Jesus to a manageable something or someone. Recall some of the books that have been all the rage in the past few years. You have Dan Brown's, *The Da Vinci Code*. Then along comes Richard Dawkin's, *The God Delusion*. Most recently we have Reza Aslan's, *Zealot*. People go wild over such books. Why? The scholarship behind them is questionable, at best. Packed with presumption and ulterior motives, they are nevertheless received with glee by people who in any and every other field would insist the authors commit to genuine scholarship and historical integrity. The authors (vainly) imagine that their popular efforts to mock Jesus and render Him toothless let them off the hook. The Jesus of the Bible is an uncomfortable reality to be avoided by the flippant and the frivolous.

Still, He stands at the end of history and draws all, big and small, to account.

Psalm 2 is all about Jesus. It exalts His Lordship over and against the taunts of the kings of this earth:

> The kings of the earth rise up and the rulers band together against the Lord and against his anointed, saying, "Let us break their chains and throw off their shackles." (vss. 2-3)

If you want to include popular authors, movie stars, university professors, and others under the category of "the kings of the earth," you are welcome to do so. The big, powerful, and influential "rise up" against God and "his anointed," that is, against the Father and His Son. Their attitude is one of defiance and independence: "We will not have this man rule over us!" and "No God—especially Jesus—is going to cramp our style!"

Check out God's response to the contempt of arrogant men:

> The One enthroned in heaven laughs; the Lord scoffs at them. (Psalm 2:4)

I think this is one of only two places in the Bible where God laughs. The other is in Psalm 37:13:

> The Lord laughs at the wicked, for he knows their day is coming.

God's response to the haughty big shots of this world is laughter. It is not that He thinks they are funny; it is that He thinks they are foolish. Imagine, mere *men* shaking a fist at God! They had sooner blow out the sun than oust the Almighty. God declares:

"I have installed my king on Zion, my holy mountain."

I will proclaim the Lord's decree:

He said to me, "You are my son; today I have become your father.

Ask me, and I will make the nations your inheritance, the ends of the earth your possession.

You will break them with a rod of iron; you will dash them to pieces like pottery."

Therefore, you kings, be wise; be warned, you rulers of the earth.

Serve the Lord with fear and celebrate his rule with trembling.

Kiss his son, or he will be angry and your way will lead to your destruction, for his wrath can flare up in a moment. Blessed are all who take refuge in him. (Psalm 2:6-12)

Hmm. It seems as though the Lord takes things a lot more seriously than the "kings of the earth" think! In Revelation, we see a day when the kings of the earth, the princes, the generals, the rich, the mighty, and everyone else—slave and free—will want to hide from Jesus Christ. These are those who mocked, ignored, ridiculed, and banished "the Lord...and his anointed."

See the scene! They call out to the very mountains: "Fall on us and hide us!" (Revelation 6:16). Suddenly, they get it. Having "suppressed the truth in unrighteousness" (*c.f.* Romans 1:18), their slumber is now over. They awaken to find reality to be very different from the dream: "They called to the mountains and the rocks, 'Fall on us and hide us from the face of him who sits on the throne and from the wrath of the Lamb! For the great day of their wrath has come, and who can withstand it?'" (Revelation 6:16-17).

Normally, there can be nothing more gentle than a lamb. Indeed, in Jesus, we see so plainly, so wonderfully, that:

> The Lord is compassionate and gracious, slow to anger, abounding in love. (Psalm 103:8)

There is no shortage of grace and patience in the Lord. This is never in question. Indeed, in Psalm 2:12, there is an invitation to one and all, including the kings of the earth, to "take refuge in him." There will never be a charge that sticks to God that He is anything less than abounding in patience and mercy.

However!

The day is coming when the Lord Jesus will strike terror into the hearts of those who have unrepentantly warred against Him. *They* will then understand what most, Christians included, these days do not: God is not to be trifled with. Yes, we rest in His arms, but we dare not slouch in His presence. *We* should tremble before our Saviour, now, even as the kings of the earth shall. The warning to the kings in Psalm 2, must not be lost on the followers of Jesus:

> Serve the Lord with fear and celebrate his rule with trembling. (Psalm 2:11)

These are fearful days! The nations are in turmoil. The evening news is enough to make the stoutest shudder...but the Christian knows better (or should). Jesus holds the trump card. Jesus has the final say in all things. It can be said that there are three types of people on earth: 1) Those who are afraid; 2) Those who do not know enough to be afraid, and; 3) Those who know Jesus. The kings of the earth will not determine the outcome of history. God will.

Dear saint, this Jesus, our Saviour, our wonderful, gentle, gracious Saviour, is one day going to display His holy, deliberate wrath against His unrepentant enemies. This is not cause for gloating, for we only stand by grace. However, it is cause for confidence—trembling confidence. It is cause for missions, not fearing those who can destroy only our bodies. It is cause for boldness against all odds. It is cause for worship…with reverence.

Here is a great mission hymn. It recognizes the Lordship of Jesus in the face of all questions. It speaks of the triumph of Jesus and His Gospel. It has, no doubt, spurred on thousands to live confidently for Christ in the face of the opposition hurled from "the kings of the earth." May it do so again today!

****

I Cannot Tell

I cannot tell why He whom angels worship,
Should set His love upon the sons of men,
Or why, as Shepherd, He should seek the wanderers,
To bring them back, they know not how or when.
But this I know, that He was born of Mary
When Bethlehem's manger was His only home,
And that He lived at Nazareth and labored,
And so the Savior, Savior of the world is come.

I cannot tell how silently He suffered,
As with His peace He graced this place of tears,
Or how His heart upon the cross was broken,
The crown of pain to three and thirty years.
But this I know, He heals the brokenhearted,
And stays our sin, and calms our lurking fear,

And lifts the burden from the heavy laden,
For yet the Savior, Savior of the world is here.

I cannot tell how He will win the nations,
How He will claim His earthly heritage,
How satisfy the needs and aspirations
Of East and West, of sinner and of sage.
But this I know, all flesh shall see His glory,
And He shall reap the harvest He has sown,
And some glad day His sun shall shine in splendor
When He the Savior, Savior of the world is known.

I cannot tell how all the lands shall worship,
When, at His bidding, every storm is stilled,
Or who can say how great the jubilation
When all the hearts of men with love are filled.
But this I know, the skies will thrill with rapture,
And myriad, myriad human voices sing,
And earth to Heaven, and Heaven to earth, will answer:
At last the Savior, Savior of the world is King!

(William Young Fullerton, 1857-1932)

Letter 9

Consider Him Who Is Awesome

Among the lampstands was someone like a son of man,
dressed in a robe reaching down to his feet and with a golden
sash around his chest. The hair on his head was white like
wool, as white as snow, and his eyes were like blazing fire.
His feet were like bronze glowing in a furnace, and his voice
was like the sound of rushing waters. In his right hand he
held seven stars, and coming out of his mouth was a sharp,
double-edged sword. His face was like the sun shining in all
its brilliance. (Revelation 1:13-16)

Dear Fellow Pilgrim,

Hamburgers are not awesome. They taste good, but they are not awesome.

Football games, by definition, cannot be awesome. They are fun, they can be thrilling, but they are not awesome.

Corndogs, movies, cars, and musicals are not awesome. Pizza is *almost* awesome, but not quite.

If you can imagine me right now, not at a computer writing, but in a pulpit preaching with all my heart, it will help me to express the passion of my heart. This subject needs some thunder behind it!

The word, *awesome*, means *inspiring or expressive of awe*. So, what does awe mean? Meriam-Webster tells us that *awe* is: *an emotion variously combining dread, veneration, and wonder that is inspired by authority or by the sacred or sublime*. Its older use takes us deeper still: *terror*. Therefore, *awesome* is *the power to inspire terror*.

Now, I like hamburgers, football, cars, and pizza. However, I cannot ever recall any of them inspiring veneration or wonder by their authority or sacredness. Corndogs have never struck terror into me. Not once. However, I hear such mundane things being heralded as "awesome" all the time. Perhaps this idolatrous age really does venerate cheesecakes as sacred and sublime. Watching a football game or a concert can certainly lead one to think a worship event is happening.

Could it be that we have made the trivial awesome and the awesome trivial?

Could it be that in making the mundane sublime, we have made the sublime mundane?

Could it be that making everything "awesome" renders nothing truly awesome?

If we let words mean what they mean, then we need to reclaim "awesome" for that which is indeed awesome and repent of the idolatry which allows the trivial to take the veneration of our hearts. To put it bluntly, the reason I just cannot see bacon or blue jeans as awesome is because I have met Jesus. Perhaps the reason so many others can is because they have not.

When you meet the awesome God, everything else takes its proper place.

I have said before, and heartily say again:

What you think about when you think about Jesus is the most important thing about you.

Without any question, we *all* need a deeper, fuller vision of Jesus—the true Jesus of the Bible. *He* is *awesome*. Therefore, all of these silly trivialities need to get off their thrones in our lives (and in our culture), and Jesus needs to reign unchallenged. Take some time to gaze at Jesus as we are presented with Him in Revelation 1:13-16. If ever there has been an awesome one, He is! Oh, how we think that Jesus is just like us, only a little bigger! We don't stand in His presence, let alone fall at His feet. We lean back in our chairs, toss our Bibles on the floor, and check Facebook…and then we call hamburgers awesome.

There is something terribly wrong with one who calls a touchdown awesome, yet snoozes through another sermon.

Awesome. The word is inappropriate except in reference to the character and works of the only one who is truly and eternally awesome.

We need a repentance revolution.

The apostle John saw Jesus in His glory. He did not yawn in His presence. He did not slouch with his feet on the sofa. Remember, this is the same John who laid his head on the chest of Jesus, His beloved Lord and friend, and heard that sinless heart beat on the last night of its earthly life (John 13:23). He was familiar with Jesus in a way that we have never been. Yet still, when he sees awesome Jesus, the Lord of Heaven…he *falls at His feet as though dead* (Revelation 1:17)!

Here is
    dread,
        veneration,
            and wonder,
                inspired by authority, the sacred, the sublime.

Now, apple pie dare not occupy such a place in your life as to bring forth dread, veneration, and wonder. It is fine to really like it. Go for a second piece if you want, but learn to *tremble* before God.

The Lord declares:

These are the ones I look on with favor: those who are humble and contrite in spirit, and who tremble at my word. (Isaiah 66:2)

So, how is your trembling going? When was the last time you considered Jesus, the Son of God, His character, and His ways and *trembled* even a little? Could it be that in ascribing to mere *things* what rightly belongs only to God, that we have lost our ability to be genuinely *awestruck*? Because ideas matter, consider with me that in giving created things the ability to do what only God can rightly do… we may be approaching blasphemy. The ability to inspire wonder, dread, and veneration belongs rightly to God, not to popcorn. The next time you designate a good parking space as "awesome," you might better think again...

Go back again to the scene in Revelation. (1:17) John, having seen the awesome one (Jesus), was stricken. He was on the floor. The next thing we see is the glorified Jesus placing His right hand on him. Rupert Bentley-Taylor pointed out that in order for the Lord Jesus to put His hand upon the prostrate John...*He had to stoop down.* The risen Lord *stooped, bent over, and got low* to comfort a trembling man. *That* is awesome. Our Lord Jesus: what a Saviour!

Beloved, is it not time for us to do some repenting? Is it not time for us to recognize we have flipped things around and made awesome the *thing* and made trivial the *maker* of the thing? Do we not need to pray for childlike wonder to be found in us again? Do we not need to learn to tremble again? Do we not need to find a proper sense of majesty again?

The place to begin is on our knees...or maybe on our faces... repenting of our idolatries and our near blasphemies. Don't be afraid to, for I think there and then you will find the risen Lord Jesus doing for you what He did for John—stooping to comfort, touching to encourage, speaking to revive.

What an awesome Lord Jesus!

Here is a hymn often sung...but oh, what words! What great truths! Don't let familiarity lead you to miss the majesty of these words, and the awesome God whom they exalt.

****

Holy, Holy, Holy!

Holy, holy, holy! Lord God Almighty!
Early in the morning our song shall rise to Thee;
Holy, holy, holy, merciful and mighty!
God in three Persons, blessed Trinity!

Holy, holy, holy! All the saints adore Thee,
Casting down their golden crowns around the glassy sea;
Cherubim and seraphim falling down before Thee,
Who was, and is, and evermore shall be.

Holy, holy, holy! though the darkness hide Thee,
Though the eye of sinful man Thy glory may not see;
Only Thou art holy; there is none beside Thee,
Perfect in power, in love, and purity.

Holy, holy, holy! Lord God Almighty!
All Thy works shall praise Thy Name, in earth, and sky, and sea;
Holy, holy, holy; merciful and mighty!
God in three Persons, blessed Trinity!

(Reginald Heber, 1783-1826)

Letter 10

Consider Him in Whose Service There Is Sweetness

I am greatly encouraged; in all our troubles my joy knows no bounds. (2 Corinthians 7:4)

Dear Friend in Jesus,

Eric Clapton has called Robert Johnson "the greatest blues guitarist of all time." The story goes that Johnson gave his soul to the Devil at a lonely, dusty crossroads in Mississippi, in return for musical talent.

Johnson lived only twenty-seven years, becoming the first of many blues/rock musicians who, strangely, died at that very age. Their names make up a gruesome Dead Rock Stars Hall of Fame:

Brian Jones, Alan Wilson, Jimi Hendrix, Jim Morrison, Janis Joplin, Peter Ham, Kurt Cobain, and Amy Winehouse, to name just a few.

The causes of death are tragic and speak of the nature of the master those musicians served:

Hanging, heroine overdose, alcohol poisoning, gunshot, vomit asphyxiation, drowning...

Whether Robert Johnson actually made a pact with Satan at that crossroads, or the story is legend, is up for debate. Regardless, we all,

Robert Johnson, you, and I, serve Satan by default, unless God does a wonderful work of grace in our lives, and we become the happy servants of Jesus:

> As for you, you were dead in your transgressions and sins, in which you used to live when you followed the ways of this world and of the ruler of the kingdom of the air, the spirit who is now at work in those who are disobedient. All of us also lived among them at one time, gratifying the cravings of our flesh and following its desires and thoughts. Like the rest, we were by nature deserving of wrath. (Ephesians 2:1-3)

The Devil is a hard master. He entices those born on his plantation into deeper service with promise after promise of pleasure and profit. Not all of his servants live hard and die young. Some will live long lives of ease and comfort. However, in the long run, the road is the same for them all: emptiness, death, and Hell. There is plenty of fine print in his gilded contract that few bother to read, but in it is found the bitter truth about what service to him really costs: He demands nothing less than your very soul.

There is no fine print in the service of Jesus, for He spells out the terms of His service from the start:

> Then he said to them all: "Whoever wants to be my disciple must deny themselves and take up their cross daily and follow me." (Luke 9:23)

> "For whoever wants to save their life will lose it, but whoever loses their life for me will save it. What good is it for someone to gain the whole world, and yet lose or forfeit their very self?" (Luke 9:24-25)

> But thanks be to God that, though you used to be slaves to sin, you have come to obey from your heart the pattern of

teaching that has now claimed your allegiance. You have been set free from sin and have become slaves to righteousness. (Romans 6:17-18)

Jesus does not in any way promise an easy servitude, but He does promise to be a loving and faithful master. There is no promise of endless pleasure, wealth, fame, or power—none of it. The cost to us is total surrender of all that we would otherwise value. Many will die young in His service. Some will be imprisoned. Others will be estranged from those who serve nature's master. The Bible makes no effort to hide this:

Then you will be handed over to be persecuted and put to death, and you will be hated by all nations because of me. (Matthew 24:9)

There were others who were tortured, refusing to be released so that they might gain an even better resurrection. Some faced jeers and flogging, and even chains and imprisonment. They were put to death by stoning; they were sawed in two; they were killed by the sword. They went about in sheepskins and goatskins, destitute, persecuted and mistreated— the world was not worthy of them. (Hebrews 11:35-38)

There is a sweetness in the service of Jesus. If you think serving Jesus is a chore, you have faulty ideas about Jesus! For the sweetness sourced in Jesus Himself. He is a wonderful Saviour, a precious friend, brother, Lord, and Master.

Our reward is nothing less than Jesus Christ Himself.

Just as we can list the many names of those who have found bitterness in the service of Satan, so we can rejoice in the names of those who have found sweetness in the service of Jesus Christ. The testimony of John G. Paton (1824-1907), the man who brought the

Gospel, at great personal expense, to the cannibals of Tanna, will not be out of place here:

> Let me record my immovable conviction that this is the noblest service in which any human being, can spend or be spent; and that, if God gave me back my life to be lived over again, I would without one quiver of hesitation lay it on the altar to Christ, that He might use it as before in similar ministries of love, especially amongst those who have never yet heard the Name of Jesus. Nothing that has been endured, and nothing that can now befall me, makes me tremble—on the contrary, *I deeply rejoice*—when I breathe the prayer that it may please the blessed Lord to turn the hearts of all my children to the Mission Field and that He may open up their way and make it *their pride and joy* to live and die in carrying Jesus and His Gospel into the heart of the Heathen World![10]

Now meet the Bishop of Smyrna, the aged and godly Polycarp. Born in A.D. 69, this follower of Jesus and disciple of the apostle John, lived for Christ under the cruelty of Rome. This good bishop was arrested in the year 155 for refusing to burn incense to the Roman emperor. One grain of incense offered to Satan's slave would have saved this old man's life, but he would have none of it. John Foxe tells the story:

> Polycarp, the venerable bishop of Smyrna, hearing that persons were seeking for him, escaped, but was discovered by a child. After feasting, [he told] the guards who apprehended him he desired an hour in prayer, which being allowed, he prayed with such fervency, that his guards repented that they had been instrumental in taking him. He was, however, carried before the proconsul, condemned, and burnt in the market place.

The proconsul then urged him, saying, "Swear, and I will release thee;—reproach Christ."

Polycarp answered, "Eighty and six years have I served him, and he never once wronged me; how then shall I blaspheme my King, Who hath saved me?" At the stake to which he was only tied, but not nailed as usual, as he assured them he should stand immovable, the flames, on their kindling the fagots, encircled his body, like an arch, without touching him; and the executioner, on seeing this, was ordered to pierce him with a sword, when so great a quantity of blood flowed out as extinguished the fire. But his body, at the instigation of the enemies of the Gospel, especially Jews, was ordered to be consumed in the pile, and the request of his friends, who wished to give it Christian burial, rejected. They nevertheless collected his bones and as much of his remains as possible, and caused them to be decently interred.[11]

As a learner of Christ I have read hundreds of biographies of those who have lived fleeting lives in the service of Jesus. Though I have read of many trials and countless hardships, there has been the consistent thread of a sweetness in Christ's service. One reads of no regrets towards Christ. One discovers the mercies and kindnesses of Jesus being multiplied in story after story. In fact, the word "sacrifice" is rarely, if ever, found on the lips of those who serve Jesus. The word "privilege" often is.

There is a sweetness in the service of Jesus that outweighs all the costs. I have recently been reminded of yet another amazing Isaac Watts hymn. I tried to fit a hymn to the theme of the chapter, but this one I have had to wedge in slightly! I trust you won't mind. This great hymn "Sweet Is the Work" refers to the "work" of praising God. Make the slight adjustment in your heart and allow this hymn to refer to the "work" of not only praising, but serving the Lord Jesus in all of life. Enjoy!

****

Sweet Is the Work

Sweet is the work, my God, my King,
To praise Thy Name, give thanks and sing,
To show Thy love by morning light
And talk of all Thy truth at night.

Sweet is the day of sacred rest,
No mortal cares shall seize my breast.
O may my heart in tune be found,
Like David's harp of solemn sound!

My heart shall triumph in my Lord
And bless His works and bless His Word.
Thy works of grace, how bright they shine!
How deep Thy counsels, how divine!

Fools never raise their thoughts so high;
Like brutes they live, like brutes they die;
Like grass they flourish, till Thy breath
Blast them in everlasting death.

But I shall share a glorious part,
When grace has well refined my heart;
And fresh supplies of joy are shed,
Like holy oil, to cheer my head.

Sin (my worst enemy before)
Shall vex my eyes and ears no more;
My inward foes shall all be slain,
Nor Satan break my peace again.

Then shall I see, and hear, and know
All I desired and wished below;

And every power find sweet employ
In that eternal world of joy.

And then what triumphs shall I raise
To Thy dear Name through endless days,
For in the realms of joy I'll see
Thy face in full felicity.

(Isaac Watts, 1674-1748)

Letter 11

Consider Him Who Is Able to Present You Faultless Before His Throne and with Great Joy!

To him who is able to keep you from stumbling and to present you before his glorious presence without fault and with great joy—to the only God our Savior be glory, majesty, power and authority, through Jesus Christ our Lord, before all ages, now and forevermore! Amen. (Jude 24-25)

Dear Friend in Jesus,

Until we have a true and proper view of the holiness of God and the depth of our sinfulness, the Gospel will never grip us with glory and joy. Our view of both is just too shallow. We take the wonder of forgiveness as a given, almost as a right. We yawn at truth which should make us shout for joy, or tremble in amazed thanksgiving.

If we can dare say "God had a problem" (and we really cannot say that, save for making this point), that problem would be forgiveness. It is simply this:

"How can a holy, sin-hating God forgive an unholy, sin-loving human?"

This is a huge problem, if viewed rightly. The Gospel is not God shrugging His shoulders at our sin and saying, "Aw shucks... don't worry about it." Grace does not say that sin does not matter. Sin matters, and the remission of sin is a "problem" for a holy God.

The problem is solved only through the life, death, and resurrection of Jesus Christ. It is only because "God made him who had no sin to be sin for us, so that in him we might become the righteousness of God" (2 Corinthians 5:21) that the otherwise insurmountable problem is solved.

However, get this: The forgiven sinner, the reigned-in rebel, the high-handed, Hell-bound catastrophe, does not merely eke into Heaven with the smell of smoke upon him. By Jesus, he is: 1) Kept from stumbling, and, 2) Presented before God's glorious presence without fault and with great joy. The tragedy becomes a trophy, and the wreck becomes a wonder.

This is the redemptive plan of Jesus.

When He saves, He really saves. He does no halfway job:

He is able to save completely those who come to God through him, because he always lives to intercede for them. (Hebrews 7:25)

He who began a good work in you will carry it on to completion until the day of Christ Jesus. (Philippians 1:6)

May your whole spirit, soul and body be kept blameless at the coming of our Lord Jesus Christ. The one who calls you is faithful, and he will do it. (1 Thessalonians 5:23-24)

Every true child of grace laments the sin that remains within him. He is deeply aware of the corruptions of his heart. This loathing of his own heart sins inevitably increases as he becomes more and more like Jesus. There can be no better news for him than that Jesus has all of this under control: His immovable purpose is to present the rebel in resplendent holiness before His throne. He will stop at nothing less, for nothing less will satisfy Him. Therefore, we should consider that if something less will satisfy us—that is, if we are content to avoid Hell, but not desirous to obtain holiness—we mean something very different by "salvation" than Jesus does. If our heart attitude is reflected in the prayer of the little girl, "God make me good...not really good, but good enough so that I don't have to get spanked," then our understanding of what we are hoping for in salvation is "sub-Christian."

However, if God has done a true work of grace in your heart, you will increasingly hate sin and love righteousness. This means you are growing in holiness. Things that once did not trouble you at all now trouble you aplenty. You are increasingly running to Jesus in confession and repentance, trusting in His blood to cleanse you. The promise that Jesus is ready, willing, and able to keep you from stumbling and present you before His glorious presence without fault and with great joy is just about the best news you have ever heard!

Jesus has promised His Father that He shall lose none of all those His Father has given to Him. He will raise them up—*each and every one*—at the last day (John 6:39). This is the will of Jesus for you. He plainly tells His Father that He wants "those you have given to me to be with me where I am, and to see my glory" (John 17:24). He is into this for His glory and your good. He is happy to present *you* as a shining example of just what He can do with a sinner.

Your destiny in Jesus is faultless character and a joyful heart, in His presence. How? How does a sinner become a faultless trophy of grace, a flawless masterpiece? The answer is found in the word, "grace." The atoning work of Jesus is so thorough, and the gift of His righteousness so complete, that the end result is a faultless presentation. None of this is of ourselves. We do not present ourselves to God, but Jesus, God the Son, does. It is His job and He does it perfectly. Therefore, we can affirm with Paul that against all odds, we have no cause for shame:

> Yet this is no cause for shame, because I know whom I have believed, and am convinced that he is able to guard what I have entrusted to him until that day. (2 Timothy 1:12)

Here are some vital questions to help you determine whether or not you are a happy subject of grace and destined for this amazing, faultless future:

- Are you trusting in Christ alone for the forgiveness of all your sins?

- Are you trusting in His gift of righteousness and no longer striving to produce your own?

- Are you seeking to hate sin in any and every form, and growing in such hatred?

- Do you hate the fact that you do not hate sin—and the fact that you do not hate the fact that you do not hate sin?

- Are you living a life of repentance, going as often as you need to the cross for cleansing?

- While despairing of your sinful self, are you rejoicing in your Saviour and His sure, saving work?

- Are you amazed and awestruck that Jesus will keep you through the storms of this life and soon present you as faultless before His throne?

Don't rush over these questions. Let them examine your heart. There is a great and wonderful Saviour. The very God we have offended is the one who invites us to Himself. What a Saviour! What a destiny! Sin shall not have the final word in the life of the simple believer. Jesus and His Gospel shall.

When old and worn, John Newton's physical faculties were all but shut down. However, this man—a prize of salvation—still certain of Jesus and His saving power, could say:

Although my memory's fading, I remember two things very clearly: I am a great sinner and Christ is a great Savior.

His great hymn, "Amazing Grace," retells the greatness of the saving work of Jesus so well. Don't let familiarity with this treasure of truth cause its power to be lost upon you. Relish these truths as though you were encountering them for the first time. They are sure to be health to your soul.

****

Amazing Grace

Amazing Grace, how sweet the sound,
That saved a wretch like me.
I once was lost but now am found,
Was blind, but now I see.

T'was Grace that taught my heart to fear.
And Grace, my fears relieved.
How precious did that Grace appear
The hour I first believed.

Through many dangers, toils and snares
I have already come;
'Tis Grace hath brought me safe thus far
and Grace will lead me home.

The Lord has promised good to me.
His word my hope secures.
He will my shield and portion be,
As long as life endures.

Yea, when this flesh and heart shall fail,
And mortal life shall cease,
I shall possess within the veil,
A life of joy and peace.

When we've been there ten thousand years
Bright shining as the sun.
We've no less days to sing God's praise
Than when we'd first begun.

(John Newton 1725-1807, stanza 6 anonymous)

Letter 12

Consider Him Who Became Poor for Our Sakes

*For you know the grace of our Lord Jesus Christ, that though
he was rich, yet for your sake he became poor, so that you
through his poverty might become rich.*
(2 Corinthians 8:9)

Dear Fellow Heir,

I am increasingly convinced that no person or council could ever have schemed the Gospel. It is beyond our invention. Religions the world over are basically the same: One and all are somehow built upon the efforts of people to obtain merit, attain to some position, or achieve some "goodness" before God or gods. Christianity *alone* belongs in another category altogether. It is about God, not people doing something to secure the salvation of those who do not deserve to be saved. It is not about merit obtained, or goodness achieved. It is about grace, the unmerited favour of God, received.

Jesus is the eternal Son of God. Along with the Father and the Holy Spirit, He "is." This is the mystery and wonder of the Trinity. You will not figure out the triune nature of God. It is beyond our understanding. If you were to invent a religion, you would not include it because it is too confounding. You would never even think of it.

Men invent religions that are minimal in mystery. There is Allah: big, unknowable, and all-powerful—period. There are the Hindu gods, myriad, and manlike. You can appease them with certain activities. You can please Allah...hopefully...with certain prescribed procedures.

There is nothing particularly profound in all this. In contrast, when you come to the Bible, you encounter God: one God, totally other, yet *with us* in Jesus, and *in us* in the Holy Spirit.

This is beyond mysterious.

We would have never thought of it. The eternal, triune nature of God had to be revealed to us in the Bible and in Jesus Christ.

Jesus, as the Son of God, has forever lived in the joy of the Father and the Holy Spirit. They have never had an argument. Together, they love being God. They love who they are and what they do. Joy, glory, and true riches are in their presence. We can barely comprehend this because we are time bound creatures of dust. When we are glorified in Heaven we will understand more, but certainly not fully plumb the depth of the nature of God.

The marvel of the Incarnation is that God the Son became a human being. On a rescue mission, Jesus Christ was born into this world. The Bible presents this as history. Indeed, the Bible belongs on the shelf with history books:

> In those days Caesar Augustus issued a decree that a census should be taken of the entire Roman world. (This was the first census that took place while Quirinius was governor of Syria.) (Luke 2:1-2)

Now, if you or I were to invent a religion, we would have the god-man born in a palace. We would gild him. He would sit on a throne and hold court. Indeed, the supposed divines of made-up religions do this very thing. But Jesus became poor. He emptied Himself of His heavenly glory and walked this dusty earth. God cried, hungered, tired, slept, and served. He had to borrow a womb to be born, and a tomb to be buried. He even had to borrow a coin for a sermon illustration. He told those who eagerly wanted to follow Him that He had no place to lay His head. He was despised, misunderstood, beaten, and scorned. Finally, He died. The Eternal Son died...not on a flowery bed of ease, but splayed upon a Roman cross.

However, just at the point when the God-Man was at His poorest, He was, in fact, rescuing those He came to save. Jesus Christ, in His dying agonies, was bearing sin and triumphing over Satan. Don't ask me how it works because I cannot tell you. I barely understand how, in the divine scheme of things, the death of God's Son accomplished the defeat of our adversary and our deliverance from sin, death, and Hell. However, the Bible says that God the Father is satisfied with the redeeming work of God the Son, and this is good enough for me.

All that Jesus gave up has now become ours. His redemptive work is so profound, so thorough, that we are now:

> Children...heirs—heirs of God and co-heirs with Christ, if indeed we share in his sufferings in order that we may also share in his glory. (Romans 8:17)

Through the poverty of Jesus, which culminated in a cross, we have been redeemed from sin and brought into the family of God. The Christian, possessing nothing, has all things. The wonders of Heaven await him, and there is within him a foretaste of the feast that is to come. The Bible uses word pictures to illustrate the indescribable riches that await us: a wedding banquet, a mansion prepared for us, streets of gold, paradise with Jesus, a feast, a crystal river, a city with gates that never close. These word images help us begin to grasp what is unimaginable. The clincher will be the very presence of God with us.

All of this has been purchased by Jesus, for us. The foretaste is now, the fullness is ahead. I am now rich in Jesus, even as a child heir is rich in the wealth of his father. All that is His is mine to have and enjoy, but more awaits. Fullness is ahead, not here and now, but there and then. My dreams and God's dreams for me require Heaven. At present, earth is too small to contain and express the riches which God has in mind for us in Christ.

We will do well to consider, rejoice in, dwell upon, speak of, and sing of our riches in Christ, both present and to come. Such will wean us from worldliness, sever the cord of materialism, free us for sacrificial service now, and wean us from the idolatrous need to get "rich" in the lower sense of the word.

About one hundred years ago, twenty-four-year-old Henry Barraclough wrote a great hymn that, unfortunately, no one sings anymore. As with so many other great hymns, it is often thought of as a bit too quaint, too flowery, or not "cool" enough. However, we are poverty-stricken Christians who really ought to just hush and learn from those who were rich in Christ. Humble yourself to be blessed by these profound words, reflective of Psalm 45.

****

Out of the Ivory Palaces

My Lord has garments so wondrous fine,
And myrrh their texture fills;
Its fragrance reached to this heart of mine
With joy my being thrills.

Out of the ivory palaces,
Into a world of woe,
Only His great eternal love
Made my Savior go.

His life had also its sorrows sore,
For aloes had a part;
And when I think of the cross He bore,
My eyes with teardrops start.

His garments too were in cassia dipped,
With healing in a touch;
Each time my feet in some sin have slipped,
He took me from its clutch.

In garments glorious He will come,
To open wide the door;
And I shall enter my heav'nly home,
To dwell forevermore.

Out of the ivory palaces,
Into a world of woe,
Only His great eternal love
Made my Savior go.

(Henry Barraclough, 1891-1983)

Letter 13

Consider Him Whose Kindness
Brings You to Repentance

Or do you show contempt for the riches of his kindness, for-bearance and patience, not realizing that God's kindness is intended to lead you to repentance? (Romans 2:4)

Friend,

We all entertain thoughts in regards to Jesus which are beneath His dignity. Our ideas matter. When we actually get into the Bible, and there meet the real Jesus, He is shocking. Failing to do this out of fear, conceit, or laziness, we are left with a caricature of Christ, to the end that we are offended by the real Jesus. Such low views give Him no glory and do us no good.

For instance, we glibly talk about Jesus' love as though He is obliged to embrace us in His saving love. He is not. He loves us because He is gracious, not because He has to. We tell ourselves that Jesus is compelled towards us because we are wonderful and lovable. That is not the case. Jesus does not love us because we are wonderful, but because He is wonderful.

Think about the kindness of Jesus. Does He have to be kind? He is *not* kind to Satan and company. He does not have to be. He is kind to us, but we are a rebel race, and if He judged it right to not be kind, who could complain? The fact that He is kind to a rebel race magnifies His marvelous nature. The wonder of the Gospel is the fact that it is not deserved. We are not cute, cuddly creatures, but violent, defiant mutineers who, given the chance, would kill God. In case you think that is too harsh, I remind you that the last time we were in fact given that chance, we took it…at Calvary.

The kindness of Jesus is not sentimental. It is not like grandmother's kindness which compels her to put extra frosting on *your* cupcake. The kindness of Jesus is deliberate and purposeful. It is exhibited not to His favourites, but to His enemies, and it has a specific goal in mind. His kindness is "cousined" with His tolerance and patience and has—for the rebel—a specific aim:

To bring the outlaw to repentance.

The kindness of Jesus is the bright diamond displayed against the dark background of a deserved wrath. This is what makes it kindness. Unless we repent, we all (without exception), are "storing up" wrath against ourselves by our stubbornness and unrepentant hearts (Romans 2:5). Things are very serious. One of the designs of Jesus Christ to bring us to repentance is His abundant kindness. He has others—warnings, trials, disciplines—but His kindness is especially targeted at bringing the rebel to his senses. This is wonderfully displayed in the most famous short story ever, the story of the wasteful son, in Luke 15. After the boy had blown all his inheritance, the remembrance of his father's kindness alone moved him towards a repentant return. You will remember that the father lavished more kindness upon his wayward son than that boy had ever imagined possible (Luke 15:17-24).

For both the follower of Jesus and the not-yet follower of Jesus, a stern warning needs to be heard here: God's kindness towards you is not to be confused with His pleasure towards you. Just because your bills are paid does not mean that Jesus is happy you are living with your girlfriend. Just because your health is restored does not mean that Jesus approves of your flirtations with the world. Our verse (Romans 2:4) tells us that He is kind so that we will stop and think, reassess, and turn around.

The thoughtless farmer in Jesus' story (Luke 12:13-21) concludes that all is well because his barns are full, when in fact, he is in grave danger with God and desperately needs to repent. He has mistaken God's kindness for God's approval, when in fact, God wholeheartedly disapproves of all he has become. What he needs to do is see the hand of God in his success and repent of his wicked, self-centred conceit.

Take a good look at your life. All around you is evidence of the abundant kindness of Jesus. His heart for you is that you be His happy, free follower, weaned from this world and subject to another; amazed at His goodness to one who has, in so many ways, shaken a fist at Him. Even towards believers in Jesus (perhaps especially towards believers), the evidence of His kindness is calculated to bring them to humility before Him.

How patient Jesus has been with me since He saved me! How kind He has been to me since He first set His saving love upon me! Certainly these kindnesses must ever bring me to a humble place before God. Certainly they must bring me not just to gratitude, but to deeper and deeper repentance. Do not make the deadly mistake of assuming that because God is kind towards you, He is happy about everything in your life. Many Gospel workers have finally foundered upon the rocks by confusing a successful season in ministry with God's approval of their lifestyles...even when sin lurked in the shadows.

"Sure I am reading a bit of porn, but God is obviously pleased with my life: I have just had the best sales year ever!" Be careful and repent! If you ignore God's voice in His kindnesses, He will speak to you in His severities.

Jesus is kind, not because you are His pet, but because He is unspeakably gracious. Don't waste His kindness. Do not show contempt for it by failing to repent of your wickedness. Think of Jesus as a surgeon who says: "Before I take that gangrenous leg off, let me try this less drastic measure." His kindness is His less drastic measure. If it brings you to the repentance He intends, He can put away His saw.

****

Come, Thou Fount of Every Blessing

Come, Thou Fount of every blessing,
Tune my heart to sing Thy grace;
Streams of mercy, never ceasing,
Call for songs of loudest praise.
Teach me some melodious sonnet,
Sung by flaming tongues above.
Praise the mount! I'm fixed upon it,
Mount of Thy redeeming love.

Sorrowing I shall be in spirit,
Till released from flesh and sin,
Yet from what I do inherit,
Here Thy praises I'll begin;
Here I raise my Ebenezer;
Here by Thy great help I've come;
And I hope, by Thy good pleasure,
Safely to arrive at home.

Jesus sought me when a stranger,
Wandering from the fold of God;
He, to rescue me from danger,
Interposed His precious blood;
How His kindness yet pursues me
Mortal tongue can never tell,
Clothed in flesh, till death shall loose me
I cannot proclaim it well.

O to grace how great a debtor
Daily I'm constrained to be!
Let Thy goodness, like a fetter,
Bind my wandering heart to Thee.
Prone to wander, Lord, I feel it,

Prone to leave the God I love;
Here's my heart, O take and seal it,
Seal it for Thy courts above.

O that day when freed from sinning,
I shall see Thy lovely face;
Clothed then in blood washed linen
How I'll sing Thy sovereign grace;
Come, my Lord, no longer tarry,
Take my ransomed soul away;
Send thine angels now to carry
Me to realms of endless day.

(Robert Robertson, 1735-1790)

Letter 14

Consider Him Who Seeks and Saves the Lost

For the Son of Man came to seek and save the lost.
(Luke 19:10)

Dear Friend,

From the beginning of the Bible, we see it is God who does the looking, we who do the hiding:

> Then the man and his wife heard the sound of the Lord God as he was walking in the garden in the cool of the day, and they hid from the Lord God among the trees of the garden. But the Lord God called to the man, "Where are you?" (Genesis 3:8-9)

What an infinite condescension! *God* looking for *us*!

Fashionable movie stars and pop culture gurus may talk passionately about how they are "on their search for god," but they have it backwards. God is the one who searches. As rebels, we hide from the light. As rebels, we do all that we can *not* to be found, while God relentlessly, graciously, lovingly pursues. We even invent religions to hide in. The reason rebels cannot find "god" is because the type of god we are looking for does not exist—a god we can shape into *our* likes and likeness, a god who agrees with *us* at all times, a god who gives peace while making no demands upon hormones or habits.

The renowned agnostic Aldous Huxley finally admitted as much:

I had motives for not wanting the world to have meaning; consequently assumed it had none, and was able without any difficulty to find satisfying reasons for this assumption. The philosopher who finds no meaning in the world is not concerned exclusively with a problem in pure metaphysics; he is also concerned to prove there is no valid reason why he personally should not do as he wants to do....For myself, as no doubt for most of my contemporaries, the philosophy of meaninglessness was essentially an instrument of liberation. The liberation we desired was simultaneously liberation from a certain political and economic system and liberation from a certain system of morality. *We objected to the morality because it interfered with our sexual freedom.*[12]

No doubt unwittingly, Huxley was here in complete agreement with Jesus Christ:

This is the verdict: Light has come into the world, but people loved darkness instead of light because their deeds were evil. Everyone who does evil hates the light, and will not come into the light for fear that their deeds will be exposed. (John 3:19-20)

The fact is that we are in hiding from God even as we claim to be on a virtuous search for reality. Presenting ourselves to be noble explorers for truth, we are in fact, rebels on the run.

Our "sincere search for God" is bogus.

Jesus, in Luke 15, likens God to a woman who has lost a coin, a shepherd who has lost a sheep, and a father who has lost a son. In each case, there is a search on; by the woman, by the shepherd, and by the father. There is no rest until there is recovery...there cannot be.

Love and faithfulness will not allow it. The little known verse says it sweetly:

> In tenderness He sought me,
> Weary and sick with sin,
> And on His shoulders brought me
> Into His flock again.
> While angels in His presence sang
> Until the courts of heaven rang.
>
> Oh, the love that sought me!
> Oh, the blood that bought me!
> Oh, the grace that brought me to the flock,
> Wondrous grace that brought me to the flock!
> (William Spencer Walton, 1850-1906)

In 1975, while a college freshman and just coming to Jesus, I was struck for the first time by the testimony of C.S. Lewis. His words still cause me to marvel at what God is like:

> You must picture me alone in that room at Magdalen, night after night, feeling, whenever my mind lifted even for a second from my work, the steady, unrelenting approach of Him whom I so earnestly desired not to meet. That which I greatly feared had at last come upon me. In the Trinity Term of 1929 I gave in, and admitted that God was God, and knelt and prayed: perhaps, that night, the most dejected and reluctant convert in all England.[13]

God does not have to be like this. He does not have to relentlessly approach us while we earnestly desire not to meet Him. If God had no choice but to look for the rebel, then the Gospel would not be founded upon grace, but obligation. If God were *obliged* to seek and save the lost by some council or principle above Him, then the Gospel would not be the Gospel, and God would not be God: free and sovereign. The wonder of this is that God seeks and saves because that is His desire. This is the grand display of His grace. His love moves Him to deal graciously with the undeserving and to go looking.

Consider your own situation:

- Do you really think that *you* looked for *Him*?

- Were *you* the first to move?

- Did *you* start the ball rolling?

- Was it *your* idea?

"Still," you say, "C.S. Lewis dreaded the approach of God, yet God hunted him down. What about commands in the Bible like, 'Seek the Lord while he may be found' (Isaiah 55:6), or the promises such as 'You will seek me and find me when you seek me with all of your heart' (Jeremiah 29:13)? Certainly such verses prove that *we*, not *God*, are the prime movers in this whole salvation caper."

This is a good observation and a good question. How do we reconcile the invitation/command to seek the Lord with the fact that God seeks us first?

Consider the case of Zacchaeus (Luke 19:1-10). Yes, Zacchaeus runs ahead and climbs a tree...but only because Jesus came to town in the first place to "seek and save that which was lost" (Luke 19:10). It is Jesus who calls out to Zacchaeus. It is Jesus who knows him by name. It is Jesus who invites himself over for lunch. It was as though Zacchaeus obeyed the call of Isaiah to "seek the Lord while he may be found" by his determination to not miss this one opportunity to see the sinners' friend as He passed. It was as though he heard the encouragement of the Lord, "You will seek me and you will find me when you seek me with all your heart" (Jeremiah 29:13), when he, in desperate determination, climbed the sycamore fig tree so he could see Jesus, his only hope.

Yes, the Bible encourages us to "seek" with the promise that we "will find," *not* because God is playing hide-and-seek, but because He is already out looking for us. *He* is the first mover. "We love because he first loved us" (1 John 4:19). However, wonder of wonders, the searching grace of God seeks out even some who, far from seeking, are on the run! Zacchaeus *wanted* Jesus and was found by Jesus. How marvelous is the grace that runs down the fleeing rebel! Let's let C.S. Lewis finish his story:

> I did not then see what is now the most shining and obvious thing; the Divine humility which will accept a convert even on such terms. The Prodigal Son at least walked home on his own feet. But who can duly adore that Love which will open the high gates to a prodigal who is brought in kicking, struggling, resentful, and darting his eyes in every direction for a chance of escape?...The hardness of God is kinder than the softness of men, and His compulsion is our liberation.[14]

What a God! What a Saviour! How we need to be humbled, amazed, *awestruck* by the grace that is in Jesus Christ! He who owes us nothing but Hell and the damnation we deserve, seeks us until He finds us. To put it perhaps more gently, more wonderfully:

> It is not he hungry seeking for bread, but Jesus, the Bread of Life seeking out the hungry. It is not the sad seeking for joy, but Jesus, the Joy of the Father, seeking out the sad. It is not emptiness seeking fullness, but Jesus, the One full of grace and truth, seeking out the empty.[15]

Here is a great old hymn which speaks of us *finding,* but more, of Christ *looking,* "ere I knew Him." I can imagine Zacchaeus singing this hymn with tears streaming down his smiling face. Oh, for the day when we sing such truths again!

****

I've Found a Friend, O Such a friend!

I've found a Friend, O such a friend! He loved me ere I knew Him;
He drew me with the cords of love, and thus He bound me to Him;
And round my heart still closely twine those ties which naught can sever,
For I am His, and He is mine, forever and forever.

I've found a Friend, O such a friend! He bled, He died to save me;
And not alone the gift of life, but His own Self He gave me!
Naught that I have mine own I call, I'll hold it for the Giver,
My heart, my strength, my life, my all are His, and His forever.

I've found a Friend, O such a friend! All pow'r to Him is given,
To guard me on my onward course, and bring me safe to heaven.
The eternal glories gleam afar, to nerve my faint endeavor;
So now to watch, to work, to war, and then to rest forever.

I've found a Friend, O such a friend! So kind and true and tender,
So wise a Counselor and Guide, so mighty a Defender!
From Him who loves me now so well what power my soul can sever?
Shall life or death, shall earth or hell? No! I am His forever.

(James G. Small, 1817-1888)

Letter 15

Consider Him Who Gives What He Commands

Then Jesus said to him, "Get up! Pick up your mat and walk." At once the man was cured; he picked up his mat and walked. (John 5:8,9)

Beloved in Christ,

One of the most meaningful books I have read is Augustine of Hippo's (A.D. 354-430) *Confessions*. The book is one entire prayer to the God who saved him...more than two hundred pages of his heart poured out to God! It reveals deep, deep soul-searching and repentance. It is a treasure trove of insight into not just the man, Augustine, but the nature of the human soul.

Deep into the volume, Augustine pours out his heart, praying:

O Love, O my God, enkindle me! Thou commandest continence; Give what Thou commandest, and command what Thou wilt.[16]

"Give what Thou commandest, and command what Thou wilt." If I flip it around, it is a bit easier to catch the power of the prayer: "Command what you will, and give what you command." This remarkably insightful prayer recognizes two truths; a disturbing one about us, a wondrous one about the Lord Jesus:

1. Our *natural inability* to do what God requires and desires. Sin has so affected each and every one of us that we are naturally unable to render the righteousness that God requires.

2. God's *gracious enabling* of us to respond to His command and do what He requires. Grace wondrously works in us, to the end that we can respond in faith and obedience to the call of Christ.

Explore these two truths with me, and then let's marvel at Jesus Christ together.

It is hard to overstate the devastation that sin has wrought upon the human race, both as a whole and as individuals. We underplay our desperate malady, thinking ourselves able to obey God naturally. However, the most humbling teachings of the Bible are, in turn, the fact of original sin, and the reality of total depravity. The first teaches that the guilt and pollution of Adam has been passed along to the whole human family. The second, that sin has affected *every* aspect of *every* person to some degree. These two, in tandem, make it impossible for us to *naturally* do what God asks of us. We cannot naturally obey Him. We cannot naturally reform ourselves. We cannot naturally come to Christ. We cannot naturally live holy lives. The reality of our inability to do what God requires of us is plainly demonstrated by the experience of all that is about us in daily life. However, more importantly, it is plainly taught in the Bible; and in no place more clearly than in the testimony of the apostle Paul:

We know that the law is spiritual; but I am unspiritual, sold as a slave to sin. I do not understand what I do. For what I want to do I do not do, but what I hate I do. And if I do what I do not want to do, I agree that the law is good. As it is, it is no longer I myself who do it, but it is sin living in me. For I know that good itself does not dwell in me, that is, in my sinful nature. For I have the desire to do what is good, but I cannot carry it out. For I do not do the good I want to do, but the evil I do not want to do—this I keep on doing. Now if I do what I do not want to do, it is no longer I who do it, but it is sin living in me that does it. So I find this law at work: Although I want to do good, evil is right there with me. For in my inner being I delight in God's law; but I see another law at work in me, waging war against the law of my mind and making me a prisoner of the law of sin at work within me. What a wretched man I am! Who will rescue me from this body that is subject to death? Thanks be to God, who delivers me through Jesus Christ our Lord! So then, I myself in my mind am a slave to God's law, but in my sinful nature a slave to the law of sin. (Romans 7:14-26)

It is equally hard to overstate the wonders of Jesus Christ who commands, but then enables. This is pure grace. This is how God works, for there can be no other way for God to work with ruined creatures but to enable; that is, to give what He commands. It has been the error of poor theologians like Pelegius (354-420)[17] and his descendant, Charles Finney, to make the street-level conclusion that a command assumes the ability to perform the command. Normally it does, except where Jesus and we are concerned! You do not tell a six-month-old to clean his room, but you do tell a six-year-old to do so... He can, so he ought. However, where things regarding our spiritual condition before a holy God are concerned, *ought* cannot imply *can* because of the dreadful reality of our depravity. Jesus has to enable, or we would have no hope whatsoever.

To help us understand the spiritual reality of Jesus enabling those dead in sin to repent, believe, follow, pursue holiness, serve, and love; Jesus, in the Gospels, repeatedly commands people to do the impossible. He commands:

- the lame to walk (Mark 2:1-12)
- the crippled to stretch forth a hand (Mark 3:1-5)
- the dead to rise (Mark 5:41)
- the dumb to speak (Mark 7:31-35)

Are these cruel jokes? Is He mocking the feeble and broken? No! These are visible pictures of what Jesus does to our spirits. He commands the lame and dead to walk and live, but then He gives what He commands. He brings life where there was death and wholeness where there was brokenness. These are but surface images of what Jesus does to the spirits of those He saves. It is what theologians call "regeneration," or what Jesus calls being "born again."

Jesus commands me to repent and believe, but then He grants new life to my dead spirit so that I can. He commands me to pursue holiness and to hate sin. Then He continually works in my heart by His Word and Spirit, bringing me to deeper and deeper repentances and humility, so that what I was, I no longer am, and what I am, is not what I will be. He commands me to love Him above all and my neighbour as myself, and then slowly and steadily works that impossible love into me.

In all of this, I have both nothing to boast of when I "do well" except the phenomenal grace of God, and no need to despair when I "do poorly," for His gracious commitment to stick with me is never in question. This whole adventure of life in Christ is begun, sustained, and guaranteed by the grace of Jesus Christ and His determination to save and sanctify all of those His Father gives Him.

None of this means that we are simply passive—far from it. The Bible is full of action commands for disciples, such as to:

- fight the good fight of the faith (2 Timothy 4:7)
- make every effort (2 Peter 1:5)
- run with perseverance (Hebrews 12:1)
- watch your life (1 Timothy 4:16)

However, even the will and ability to fight, run, or watch, are gifts of God in His graciousness. Though not naturally in us, graciously they are given to us.

Augustine's prayer applies across every aspect of the Christian life, but was particularly prayed in reference to *continence*, that is, sexual restraint and purity. Augustine had lived a very promiscuous life for years before his conversion at age thirty-two. He had a mistress whom he adored. When he was grabbed by the Gospel and saved, sexual purity must have seemed like an impossibility to him. Indeed, most modern "disciples" would just assume its impossibility and excuse their unchastity: "God cannot expect me to suppress my passions!" Well, yes, He can, because He "gives what He commands".

Augustine reasoned that, not being his place to modify the clear commands of Christ to live a holy life (as we would today), it *must* be in the mind and heart of God to enable the otherwise unable! The follower of Jesus who battles against his homosexual desires, the Christian husband who lives faithfully with a tragically handicapped and sexually unable wife, the single disciple with no legitimate sexual possibilities, the man with porn addiction in his past—all, *all* are called to sexual purity against whatever odds, *because* Christ will give what He commands.

There is now hope.

There is now no room for our lame excuses.

Watch out! The wondrous fact that the Lord Jesus will give you the power to will and do what He commands is a litmus test for the state of your heart. If this fact thrills you as it fills you with hope, then your heart may well be healthy. If it disturbs and annoys you because it just demolished your excuses, then you may be in great danger.

> To him who is able to keep you from stumbling and to present you before his glorious presence without fault and with great joy—to the only God our Savior be glory, majesty, power and authority, through Jesus Christ our Lord, before all ages, now and forevermore! Amen. (Jude 24-25)

> May God himself, the God of peace, sanctify you through and through. May your whole spirit, soul and body be kept blameless at the coming of our Lord Jesus Christ. The one who calls you is faithful, and he will do it. (1 Thessalonians 5:23-24)

The precious hymn below by the little known Elvina Hall, expresses so beautifully the truth that Jesus enables the unable. Knowing the smallness of our strength, our Saviour, through the richness of His atoning grace, not only pardons but can and will "change the leper's spots and melt the heart of stone."

****

Jesus Paid It All

I hear the Savior say,
"Thy strength indeed is small;
Child of weakness, watch and pray,
Find in Me thine all in all."

> *Jesus paid it all,*
> *All to Him I owe;*
> *Sin had left a crimson stain,*
> *He washed it white as snow.*

For nothing good have I
Whereby Thy grace to claim,
I'll wash my garments white
In the blood of Calv'ry's Lamb.

And now complete in Him
My robe His righteousness,
Close sheltered 'neath His side,
I am divinely blest.

Lord, now indeed I find
Thy power and Thine alone,
Can change the leper's spots
And melt the heart of stone.

When from my dying bed
My ransomed soul shall rise,
"Jesus died my soul to save,"
Shall rend the vaulted skies.

And when before the throne
I stand in Him complete,
I'll lay my trophies down
All down at Jesus' feet.

> *Jesus paid it all,*
> *All to Him I owe;*
> *Sin had left a crimson stain,*
> *He washed it white as snow.*

(Elvina Hall, 1822-1889)

Letter 16

Consider Him Who Created Mangoes

Through him all things were made; without him nothing was
made that has been made. (John 1:3)

Dear Fellow Marveler,

Jesus did not have to be so amazingly, wondrously creative. Or perhaps, He did. Maybe the very heart of God is compelled to manifest
itself in a myriad of colours, millions of species of living things, endless galaxies containing who-knows-what wonders, a profusion of
textures and smells and flavours…and mangoes,…all to the praise of
His glory, and for our joy.

Personally, I think that Jesus, *through whom all things were made,*
outdid Himself when He made mangoes. How can someone be an
atheist with a glorious, sweet, intense mango in his mouth, juice drip-
ping right down his hands and arms and off his elbows? All creation,
properly considered, is calculated by God to produce worship in
humans (Psalm 19:1-2).

Bonhoeffer was right when he proposed that every meal eaten
should be an act of worship for the Christian.

> Every mealtime [should!] fills Christians with gratitude for
> the living, present Lord and God, Jesus Christ…in their whole-
> hearted joy in the good gifts of this physical life, [Christians]
> acknowledge their Lord as the true giver of all good gifts; and
> beyond this, as the true Gift; the true Bread of life itself; and
> finally, as the One who is calling them to the banquet of the

Kingdom of God. So, in a singular way, the daily table fellowship binds the Christians to their Lord and one another... God cannot endure that unfestive, mirthless attitude of ours in which we eat our bread in sorrow, with pretentious, busy haste, or even with shame. Through our daily meals He is calling us to rejoice, to keep holiday in the midst of our working day.[18]

This truth is just a subset to the greater truth that all of life is to be an act of worship for the believer:

And whatever you do, whether in word or deed, do it all in the name of the Lord Jesus, giving thanks to God the Father through him. (Colossians 3:17)

True Christian spirituality sees no sacred/secular divide. The earth is the Lord's, and therefore, every aspect of life for the Christian is of deep spiritual significance. Cutting the grass, making love to one's spouse, earning money, eating a mango, for the Christian, all these are done within the horizon of Jesus' Lordship just as certainly as are taking the bread and wine, and devoutly reading the Bible.

Remembering that ideas matter, just think about what a mango says about Jesus:

- It tells us He is immeasurably creative. He could have made *one* flavour, *one* colour, *one* texture, but no, not Jesus! No wonder the angels erupted in joyful praise when Jesus was creating (*c.f.* Job 38:6-8)! How could they not?

- It tells us that He is wondrously gracious. He did not have to give us taste buds, olfactory membranes, or cones and rods. Life could have been bland and colourless, but not with Jesus behind it all!

- It tells us that He is rich in delights. Jesus is no austere, stern, stingy killjoy. He is the original partier: all fun, joy, and delight come from Him. All that Satan can do is produce poor and perverse imitations. Jesus is the author of delight.

I remember helping a seventy-five-year-old man come to Jesus. He had been a rough and ready Royal Marine. He had known the hard life, the "good" life, and then the new life. When he came to Jesus, he told me that his world changed from black and white to colour. That is what Jesus does!

Believe me when I tell you that flavours become sweeter, sunsets deeper, colours brighter, laughter richer, tears more precious, romance more profound, and trials more meaningful when Jesus is finally seen and worshipped as the source of it all. Love intensifies and life deepens when Jesus is Lord. Every "thing" becomes, less meaningful and more meaningful—both at the same time. A meal, a bird in a tree, a star in the night sky, an amazing play on the sports field—all are nothing compared to Jesus, and yet all are immeasurably enriched by the presence of Jesus. The kiss of a spouse, a walk with a friend, the sanctuary of the deathbed all become—at the very same time—both of transitory value and permanent significance. The Christian lets go of everything and gains everything—both at the same time. He holds all things loosely, yet with a newfound preciousness. This is what Jesus does to life. Everything takes a new place *under* His Lordship.

The Bible makes it clear that all things were made by and for Jesus:

All things have been created through him and for him. (Colossians 1:16)

It also makes it clear that all things are given for us to enjoy:

God...richly provides us with everything for our enjoyment. (1 Timothy 6:17)

It saddens and concerns me that we are so quickly losing our ability to be amazed. When my father was a boy, a wheel and a stick with which to roll it, were his delightful toys. (I still see this simple pleasure among children in "poor" countries the world over.) Today, we are so overstimulated that things which should cause us to be deeply satisfied, erupt in praise, bow in silent adoration, or respond with amazed thanksgiving, seem to go unnoticed and unappreciated. When was the last time you *worshipped* or were *awestruck* by a meal, a conversation, or a crescent moon? When was the last time something of the goodness, artistry, generosity, or graciousness of God washed over you as you felt, tasted, smelled, saw, laughed, cried, conversed, held, or romanced? When a mango causes me to worship Jesus, who made the mango and gave me the ability to enjoy it, my world is right side up. When I eat the mango without the amazed worship of Jesus Christ, I am simply a modern Epicurean,[19] a gross idolater, with my world upside down, heading for a crash.

How wonderful is the Lord Jesus! How rich, gracious, expressive, creative, generous, and delightful! How vast and wide and high and long is His love in all its expressions and nuances! How indescribably rich and strange is the heavenward life lived with Jesus, where the simplest things (mangoes and embraces) become profound reasons to praise and worship, and the most "advanced" things (glittering gadgets and gizmos) become comparatively meaningless and insignificant; where one has given up all, yet possesses everything to enjoy.

Don't try to be more spiritual than God has made you to be. We are neither ascetic monks nor godless pagans. We dare not lose the ability to be spellbound, amazed, and blessed by what others around us consider to be humdrum, or the super spiritual consider to be profane. We know better. The deep purple in the sunset tells us something of the wonders of our God, as does the smell of the winter fire, or the crack of the ball on the bat in springtime.

> Till you can sing and rejoice and delight in God, as misers do
> in gold, and kings in scepters, you will never enjoy the world.
> (Thomas Traherne)

****

Joyful, Joyful, We Adore Thee

Joyful, joyful, we adore Thee, God of glory, Lord of love;
Hearts unfold like flowers before Thee, opening to the sun above.
Melt the clouds of sin and sadness; drive the dark of doubt away;
Giver of immortal gladness, fill us with the light of day!

All Thy works with joy surround Thee, earth and heaven reflect Thy rays,
Stars and angels sing around Thee, center of unbroken praise.
Field and forest, vale and mountain, flowery meadow, flashing sea,
Singing bird and flowing fountain call us to rejoice in Thee.

Thou art giving and forgiving, ever blessing, ever blessed,
Wellspring of the joy of living, ocean depth of happy rest!
Thou our Father, Christ our Brother, all who live in love are Thine;
Teach us how to love each other, lift us to the joy divine.

Mortals, join the happy chorus, which the morning stars began;
Father love is reigning o'er us, brother love binds man to man.
Ever singing, march we onward, victors in the midst of strife,
Joyful music leads us Sunward in the triumph song of life.

(Henry van Dyke, 1852-1933)

Letter 17

Consider Him Who Will No Longer
Send You to Hell

As far as the east is from the west, so far has he removed our transgressions from us. (Psalm 103:12)

Dear Friend in Jesus,

If God were for one minute to withdraw His mercy from any member of this sinful race, they would surely and justly perish forever for their crimes and sins against God.

The "natural" man (any human being who has not received the supernatural saving mercy of God), is on a sure and deserved path to destruction. He lives to breathe one more breath by the sheer mercy of God. Hell gapes beneath him as surely as the sky hangs above him. While he may flatter himself with the notion, "*If* God happens to exist after all, He would not dare judge me," he is in fact on a slippery path, upheld moment by moment by the patience and goodness of the God he has a thousand times offended. Ideas matter, and ideas about God matter the most.

This is what the Bible plainly teaches:

It is mine to avenge; I will repay.
    In due time their foot will slip;
their day of disaster is near
    and their doom rushes upon them. (Deuteronomy 32:35)

Whoever believes in the Son has eternal life, but whoever rejects the Son will not see life, for God's wrath remains on them. (John 3:36)

As for you, you were dead in your transgressions and sins.... Like the rest, we were by nature deserving of wrath. (Ephesians 2:1-3)

Surely you place them on slippery ground;
   you cast them down to ruin.
How suddenly are they destroyed,
   completely swept away by terrors!
They are like a dream when one awakes;
   when you arise, Lord,
   you will despise them as fantasies. (Psalm 73:18-20)

On July 8, 1741 in Enfield Connecticut, a sober-minded Jonathan Edwards told a conscience stricken congregation that without the mercies of Jesus, they

...have no refuge, nothing to take hold of...all that preserves them every moment is the...uncovenanted, unobliged forbearance, of an incensed God.[20]

These days we find such words shocking. Our view of God is so deflated and our view of ourselves so inflated that consequently we live in the pale light of a dulled and diminished "gospel." We flatter ourselves with foolish thoughts that we really are good at the core, better in the heart than may appear on the surface, not that different from God (who does not *really* hate sin (at least not *ours*) anyway), and that we are therefore in no real, imminent, eternal danger. The sobering teaching of the Bible is that we are rebels, ruined by our own sin, enslaved to our corruption, and in certain danger of judgment from a white-hot, holy God. If we do not flat-out deny this truth, we at least file it deeply away and all but forget it, lest we embarrass ourselves before our sophisticated colleagues or backstreet buddies.

The modern "gospel" is, more often than not, seen as just an offering from a friendly God to make us more comfortable, to brighten our day, or to spice up our already spiffy lives. The thought that the Gospel is actually the only and urgent remedy for wrecked rebels—Hell-deserving vessels of wrath, doomed to destruction—is just considered to be too strong for our modern, tender palates.

However, this is what the Bible plainly teaches.

The Gospel displays its depth and riches against this backdrop of very real depravity and impending doom. It is against this dark background that the wonders of our salvation come into glorious view.

I'll *try* to explain!

In the Gospel, God *covenants*—promises in blood—to avert His wrath from those deserving of it, only to pour it out upon Himself in the person of His Son Jesus. It is deadly serious business. Without the Gospel, we exist moment by moment by the "uncovenanted, unobliged forbearance, of an incensed God." Aside from and outside of the mercies of Jesus Christ, we are ripe for judgment. We deserve it. However, something happens when Jesus Christ comes into the picture.

We need to get this, so be ready to *think*: Because of the saving work of Jesus Christ, we no longer just *avoid* the wrath of God...we no longer *deserve* the wrath of God. I hope that has shocked you. It needs to. It needs to never stop shocking us. The Gospel should take our breath away.

First, apart from Jesus, we all deserve the just wrath of a holy God. God is under no obligation to give us our next breath, and He is both just and right to judge, punish, and condemn the unrepentant.

Second, God was under no obligation to us to provide a just and holy way to deal with our sins, other than damning us. However, out of His merciful grace toward undeserving sinners, He has, in fact, provided another way for us to be just and holy (wonder of wonders!) through the death of Jesus Christ on the cross.

Finally, in the Gospel, *forgiveness* is much more than God not giving us what our sins deserve. Gospel forgiveness says more than: "You deserve judgment, but I am not going to judge you, because I forgive you." It says more than: "I am not going to give you what you deserve." As amazing as not getting what we deserve is, the Gospel offers more, much more. The Gospel says that not only are we *not* given the judgment we *do* deserve, but we are *justified*, that is, *declared righteous before God.* We are given a righteousness we *do not* deserve and *reconciled* to God, that is, brought back into a relationship with our Father. Gospel forgiveness says more than: "I won't punish you. You can go your way." Gospel forgiveness says: "You are cleansed and clothed, righteous and reconciled. Come to me."

So, do we *deserve* to be damned? Yes and no.

Yes: Without Jesus, on my own, with no covenant relationship with God, relying upon my own righteousness—without argument—I deserve to be damned.

No: With Jesus, I am justified before a holy God. This means that the very ground for accusation has been removed, and I am now righteous before the Father, in and through Jesus. My whole position has changed.

To put it another, more daring way: Through the wondrous work of Jesus on the cross, God has changed His mind in regard to me. The rebel has been reconciled. The wicked one has been justified. The sinner has been declared righteous.

For the believer, God is no longer:

* Uncovenanted. We are now in a covenant of grace with our Father, purchased and secured by His Son Jesus.

Then he took a cup, and when he had given thanks, he gave it to them, saying, "Drink from it, all of you. This is my blood of the covenant, which is poured out for many for the forgiveness of sins." (Matthew 26:27-28)

- Unobliged. His own Word and promises oblige Him to forgive and welcome those who come to Him through Christ.

For I have come down from heaven not to do my will but to do the will of him who sent me. And this is the will of him who sent me, that I shall lose none of all those he has given me, but raise them up at the last day. For my Father's will is that everyone who looks to the Son and believes in him shall have eternal life, and I will raise them up at the last day. (John 6:38-40)

- Incensed. Christ's work on the cross has reconciled the rebel to the King (the Father). The war is over. The relationship is restored.

All this is from God, who reconciled us to himself through Christ...that God was reconciling the world to himself in Christ, not counting people's sins against them. (2 Corinthians 5:18-19)

To the poverty of our souls and of our worship, our ruin is so much greater and our salvation so much deeper than we have understood. I am going to give you a buffet of Scripture passages below, so you might see I am not making any of this up.

God made him who had no sin to be sin for us, so that in him we might become the righteousness of God. (2 Corinthians 5:21)

Therefore, there is now no condemnation for those who are in Christ Jesus. (Romans 8:1)

He does not treat us as our sins deserve
    or repay us according to our iniquities.
For as high as the heavens are above the earth,
    so great is his love for those who fear him;

as far as the east is from the west,
so far has he removed our transgressions from us. (Psalm
103:10-12)

Therefore, since we have been justified through faith, we have
peace with God through our Lord Jesus Christ. (Romans 5:1)

For he has rescued us from the dominion of darkness and
brought us into the kingdom of the Son he loves, in whom we
have redemption, the forgiveness of sins. (Colossians 1:13-14)

The Lord your God is with you,
    the Mighty Warrior who saves.
He will take great delight in you;
    in his love he will no longer rebuke you,
    but will rejoice over you with singing. (Zephaniah 3:17)

But you are a chosen people, a royal priesthood, a holy nation,
God's special possession, that you may declare the praises of
him who called you out of darkness into his wonderful light.
Once you were not a people, but now you are the people of
God; once you had not received mercy, but now you have
received mercy. (1 Peter 2:9-10)

What is more, I consider everything a loss because of the sur-
passing worth of knowing Christ Jesus my Lord, for whose
sake I have lost all things. I consider them garbage, that I may
gain Christ and be found in him, not having a righteousness
of my own that comes from the law, but that which is through
faith in Christ—the righteousness that comes from God on the
basis of faith. (Philippians 3:8-9)

I belong to my beloved, and his desire is for me. (Song of
Songs 7:10)

The Scripture listing could go on and on, trip after trip to the buffet table of God's rich truth! My heart's aim is that we adore something of the depth of the love of God through Jesus Christ...so much more, so much deeper than perhaps we had thought. Oh that God's Holy Spirit would work in our minds and hearts to the end that the wonders of our salvation would transform and overwhelm our lives!

For this reason I kneel before the Father, from whom every family in heaven and on earth derives its name. I pray that out of his glorious riches he may strengthen you with power through his Spirit in your inner being, so that Christ may dwell in your hearts through faith. And I pray that you, being rooted and established in love, may have power, together with all the Lord's holy people, to grasp how wide and long and high and deep is the love of Christ, and to know this love that surpasses knowledge—that you may be filled to the measure of all the fullness of God. (Ephesians 3:13-19)

I hope there will be a Cornish Male Voice Choir in Heaven (complete with Billy Bray and Henry Martyn!) singing the great salvation hymn below.

****

I Hear Thy Welcome Voice

I hear Thy welcome voice
That calls me, Lord, to Thee,
For cleansing in Thy precious blood
That flowed on Calvary.

> *I am coming Lord!*
> *Coming now to Thee!*
> *Wash me, cleanse me in the blood*
> *That flowed on Calvary!*

Though coming weak and vile,
Thou dost my strength assure;
Thou dost my vileness fully cleanse,
Till spotless all, and pure.

'Tis Jesus calls me on
To perfect faith and love,
To perfect hope and peace and trust,
For earth and Heav'n above.

'Tis Jesus Who confirms
The blessèd work within,
By adding grace to welcomed grace,
Where reigned the power of sin.

And He the witness gives
To loyal hearts and free
That every promise is fulfilled,
If faith but brings the plea.

All hail! atoning blood!
All hail! redeeming grace!
All hail! the gift of Christ our Lord,
Our Strength and Righteousness!

> *I am coming Lord!*
> *Coming now to Thee!*
> *Wash me, cleanse me in the blood*
> *That flowed on Calvary*

(Lewis Hartsough, 1826-1919)

Letter 18

Consider Him Who Wins Through Losing

*But I am a worm and not a man, scorned by everyone,
despised by the people.* (Psalm 22:6)

Dear Ones,

I have already said (but dare say again), that neither you nor I could ever have conceived the wonders of the Gospel. It just goes against the norm time and time again. In it, God does not operate in expected ways , or in the ways we ourselves act.

There are five key images or scenes in the Bible that help us to understand the incredible richness of our salvation in Jesus:

- The *Courtroom.* Here the guilty sinner is *justified* before a holy judge through the sin-bearing of the innocent one, Jesus.

- The *Slave Market.* Here the one in bondage to sin and Satan is *redeemed* and set free through the payment of the free one, Jesus.

- The *Family.* Here the estranged and unfaithful rebel is *reconciled* to his loving Father and family through the intercession of the faithful one, Jesus.

- The *Temple.* Here the wrath of God toward the wicked one is *propitiated* through the sacrifice of the righteous one, Jesus.

- The *Battlefield.* Here the evil one is *defeated* through the victory of the triumphant one, Jesus.

Each of these scenes portrays a vital aspect of our salvation in Jesus, and each has as its foundation, the self-substitution of Jesus Christ on the cross for us, sinners. Considering each of these realities of our salvation will greatly enrich our understanding of just what God—Father, Son, and Holy Spirit—has accomplished for us through the cross. Together, they form a fuller picture of what Jesus has done for us than any single image can do on its own.

I want to focus on *one* image in this letter—that of the *battle-field*. Historically, this image has been called *Christus Victor.* Unfortunately, due to an overemphasis of this aspect of Christ's work on the cross by some,[21] many of us have underplayed this vital and wonderful truth relating to our salvation: Jesus, through the cross, has triumphed for us over our enemy, Satan. There are a great number of scriptures that speak of Jesus' victory through the cross, but for the sake of time, I will focus on two.

To begin, we need to agree that there is no greater picture of losing and weakness than Jesus on the cross. Calvin Miller, speaking of the crucified Christ writes:

> He did not come across to any casual Roman observer as a man who was winning. When you are forced to die naked in front of your own mother, it can make you seem a loser with none on earth to vouch for your character.[22]

Here is Jesus, losing His very life. Here is Jesus at His weakest. Here is the Incarnate Son of God at His lowest point. Here He is as "a worm and not a man," and "a sheep before his shearers." Can this be a picture of triumph? How? I cannot comprehend, let alone explain, the depths of the mystery of the cross in its various aspects. However, with trembling pen, I can venture to explore and explain the fringes of our salvation.

Come with me to the last week of Jesus' life. Jesus is looking towards the cross. Hear His sacred words:

> Jesus replied, "The hour has come for the Son of Man to be glorified. Very truly I tell you, unless a kernel of wheat falls to the ground and dies, it remains only a single seed. But if it dies, it produces many seeds. Anyone who loves their life will lose it, while anyone who hates their life in this world will keep it for eternal life. Whoever serves me must follow me; and where I am, my servant also will be. My Father will honor the one who serves me. (John 12:23-26)

> "Now my soul is troubled, and what shall I say? 'Father, save me from this hour'? No, it was for this very reason I came to this hour. Father, glorify your name!"

> Then a voice came from heaven, "I have glorified it, and will glorify it again." The crowd that was there and heard it said it had thundered; others said an angel had spoken to him.

> Jesus said, "This voice was for your benefit, not mine. Now is the time for judgment on this world; now the prince of this world will be driven out. And I, when I am lifted up from the earth, will draw all people to myself." He said this to show the kind of death he was going to die. (John 12:23-33)

When He uttered the words, "the hour has come," without question Jesus was referring to His own death on the cross. He tells us plainly that through His willing weakness, He will be glorified, the Father's name will be glorified, this sinful world system will be judged, and the evil prince of this world will be driven out.

The above scriptures are all winning words of victory and confidence, but none more so than that great declaration: *"prince of this world will be driven out."* This is a declaration of inevitable victory. Satan is going to be driven out through the death of Jesus on a Roman cross. Here deep wonders are being spoken of—deeper than we can plumb. You do not have to fully understand this in order to believe it and receive it. However, grasp this wondrous truth: Somehow, in the ways and wonders of God, Jesus Christ absorbed the wrath of God and redeemed, reconciled, and justified the wicked. Through the death of Christ in which He was substituted for sinners, Satan, our ancient adversary and accuser, is soundly defeated. The Son of God, in weakness, in crucifying tortures, deals with sin in all its aspects and consequences and in so doing, defeats the enemy of our souls.

Next, come with me to the cross itself. How thankful we can be that the Holy Spirit made sure that this remarkable scene is in the Bible!

One of the criminals who hung there hurled insults at him: "Aren't you the Messiah? Save yourself and us!" But the other criminal rebuked him. "Don't you fear God," he said, "since you are under the same sentence? We are punished justly, for we are getting what our deeds deserve. But this man has done nothing wrong."

Then he said, "Jesus, remember me when you come into your kingdom."

Jesus answered him, "Truly I tell you, today you will be with me in paradise." (Luke 23:39-43)

If ever Satan thought he had a soul in his grip, it would have been here! Look: A criminal...a guilty, wicked *sinner*...at death. What hope can there be for him? He turns to Jesus...not a glowing, resplendent

Jesus, but a naked, gasping, bleeding Jesus. What power can there be in such a Jesus? Even the criminal's "prayer" is a mere and weak nine words long... Having said that, J.C. Ryle found no less than *eight* profound truths in this nine-word prayer: 1) The soul survives the body; 2) There is a world to come; 3) Christ has a kingdom; 4) That kingdom is better than this present evil world; 5) Jesus Christ will share that kingdom with sinners; 6) Entrance to that kingdom requires repentance; 7) Christ, though dying in weakness, has power to open doors to the kingdom; 8) Trusting in Christ is essential to salvation.[23] Wow!

A pitiful scene for sure...but what a triumph!

In this scene we see that the power of Jesus, even at His weakest, is able to do what no other, even at his strongest, can ever do: Erase the sins of the rebel, grant him the gift of eternal life, and snatch his mutinous soul from the clutches of Hell itself. Satan's designs for that criminal were utterly destroyed by Jesus. Jonathan Edwards wrote:

> The weapon with which Christ warred against the devil, and obtained the most complete victory and glorious triumph over him, was the cross, the instrument and weapon with which he thought he had over-thrown Christ, and brought on him shameful destruction...In his last sufferings, Christ sapped the very foundations of Satan's kingdom; he conquered his enemies in their own territories, and beat them with their own weapons; as David cut off Goliath's head with his own sword.[24]

In *losing* all that we would think of as power, strength, authority, and might, Jesus Christ *wins* the battle over sin and Satan and releases countless sinners from their enemy.

Did you know that your very soul is a battlefield? Indeed, your soul has an enemy. Ah, but your soul has a friend. There is one who wills to destroy you, but one who wills to save you: Jesus Christ. He has decidedly triumphed, and has defeated your adversary through His seeming loss on the cross.

Be ever sure that you walk in the victory that Christ won for you on that cruel hill outside of Jerusalem so many years ago. Satan's final doom is sure, for the decisive battle has been fought and won.

Worship Jesus Christ, your victorious Saviour!

****

All Hail the Power of Jesus' Name!

All hail the power of Jesus' Name! Let angels prostrate fall;
Bring forth the royal diadem, and crown Him Lord of all.
Bring forth the royal diadem, and crown Him Lord of all.

Let highborn seraphs tune the lyre, and as they tune it, fall
Before His face Who tunes their choir, and crown Him Lord of all.
Before His face Who tunes their choir, and crown Him Lord of all.

Crown Him, ye morning stars of light, who fixed this floating ball;
Now hail the strength of Israel's might, and crown Him Lord of all.
Now hail the strength of Israel's might, and crown Him Lord of all.

Crown Him, ye martyrs of your God, who from His altar call;
Extol the Stem of Jesse's Rod, and crown Him Lord of all.
Extol the Stem of Jesse's Rod, and crown Him Lord of all.

Ye seed of Israel's chosen race, ye ransomed from the fall,
Hail Him Who saves you by His grace, and crown Him Lord of all.
Hail Him Who saves you by His grace, and crown Him Lord of all.

Hail Him, ye heirs of David's line, whom David Lord did call,
The God incarnate, Man divine, and crown Him Lord of all,
The God incarnate, Man divine, and crown Him Lord of all.

Sinners, whose love can ne'er forget the wormwood and the gall,
Go spread your trophies at His feet, and crown Him Lord of all.
Go spread your trophies at His feet, and crown Him Lord of all.

Let every tribe and every tongue before Him prostrate fall
And shout in universal song the crownèd Lord of all.
And shout in universal song the crownèd Lord of all.

O that, with yonder sacred throng, we at His feet may fall,
Join in the everlasting song, and crown Him Lord of all,
Join in the everlasting song, and crown Him Lord of all!

(Edward Perronet, 1726-1792; last verse added by John Rippon, 1751-1836)

Letter 19

Consider Him Who Delights in Reducing You

In the course of my life, he broke my strength. (Psalm 102:23)

Dear Ones,

We simply have to be broken. There is no choice. We are too crooked, and as we are Jesus cannot use us. As things stand, He cannot be our soul's delight. We must be reduced to a heap of rubble before a loving Jesus, so that He can remake us.

Jesus does not delight in reducing us because He is a sadist. There is not something wrong with Jesus. However, there is much wrong with us. Our values, priorities, and systems are all twisted and contorted. His delight is not that of a madman, but of the all wise King of Love. It is a delight with a glorious end in view. Even at its toughest, there is a tenderness to it.

We need to admit that if we had things our way, we would choose pathways of ease. The ascent would be gradual and pretty. Any descents would be momentary and manageable. Life would be an easy layup. Our growth in Christlikeness would not involve anything like Jesus' self-emptying. Most of us would opt for some sort of sanctification which would fit into our lives with as little disruption as possible. If we could somehow access a drive-through that dispensed character, we would do it: "Just place your order at the smiling clown to collect peace, patience, or happiness. Then drive around the corner and pick it up at the next window!"

The fact is that Christian character comes at a price. That price is brokenness. Many of us, when we come to Christ, perversely think of ourselves as a great addition to Jesus and His cause: *How did the Kingdom of God ever get on without me?* We wrongly think it is our natural giftedness that Jesus was looking for when He chased after us—indeed—that *He* needed *us* more than *we* needed *Him*!

There are at least two major problems with such thinking (besides the fact that it is arrogant and foolish):

First, it keeps us from truly treasuring Jesus, for it is those who have been forgiven much who love much (*c.f.* Luke 7:47). The self-confident, self-assured, self-righteous, self-_____ (fill in the blank) never can appreciate Jesus, the friend of sinners: Jesus, the one who makes princesses out of scrub girls; Jesus, the one who gives strength to the weary; Jesus, the one who binds up the brokenhearted; Jesus, the one who gives life to the dead.

The one who is "doing Christ a favour" is more often than not an arrogant religionist—Evangelical and orthodox perhaps, but not desperate. It is when the misguided zealot becomes the desperate disciple that Jesus becomes immeasurably precious. This desperation requires brokenness. It requires that one be brought to the end of oneself. Jesus is only treasured when we get to the place where we experientially *feel* that we are absolutely undone without Him.

Second, off-centre thinking keeps us from operating in the supernatural gifting and purpose of God. Our natural giftedness, more often than not, keeps us from the meaningful life Jesus has planned and purposed for us. As long as we think we can do "it," "it" will not be very amazing...at least not in an eternally significant way. "It" may mean becoming great in the eyes of a Hell-bound culture, but that can mean a wasted life in terms of eternity. Even when God does use our natural abilities, He usually brings us to a place where we lose our ease and confidence with them, and have to rely upon His grace and power to use them, for they were not ours in the first place. Therefore, even our natural strengths bear testimony not to us, but to Him.

Calvin Miller rightly observed: "Christ aims to make us useful, Satan to make us a star."[25] Christ also aims to make us adore His mercies and goodness. Make us? Yes, *make us.* For in *making* us useful to Him and adoring of Him, He is actually doing us a great favour. We are too sinful and "self-everything" to make ourselves useful to Him, or adoring of Him who wills us only the best. So *make us* He must, because we will never make ourselves.

The making can be (and usually is) painful. The process may take years, punctuated with seasons of breaking. The proud dad, gloating over "his" amazing kids (implying: "Look what a great father I am!") may need to endure the breaking that only a rebellious child can bring. The powerful preacher, easily able to proclaim Christian truth, with a full schedule and demands and invitations pouring in, may have to live through the "death" of losing all public confidence, complete with the horror of public panic attacks. Perhaps a few health problems will need to be added to the mix, and some indescribably painful betrayals. The end result is a broken person, but a better person, a thankful, desperate servant and friend of Jesus.

C.S. Lewis observed that he didn't go to Christianity to make himself happy, knowing that a bottle of Port would do that. He asserted that if one wants a religion to make one feel really comfortable, Christianity was not the recommended choice! I recently came across an interesting quote from Jack Nicholson. Like most of what comes out of Hollywood, it is pure foolishness, but plays to my point:

> I don't believe in God now...I can still work up an envy for someone who has a faith. I can see how that could be a deeply soothing experience.

A deeply soothing experience? Oh, Jack! If only you knew! Not when Jesus gets involved!

Remember when you prayed to be made more like Jesus? What did you think you were asking God to do? Read the Gospels. Jesus did not have a luxury life, but a life of continual breaking, culminating in the crushing of Gethsemane, where He submitted to all the Father had (and has) for Him, with these sanctified words: "Yet not what I will, but what you will." (Mark 14:36). Even then there is no record of the Father ever answering, but just accepting the submission of His Son.

The key is not to kick against Jesus' grand purpose when the breaking is taking place. He *has* to do it, if we are to become the people *He* intends for us to be. The real deep work may not take place at the huge, exciting Christian gathering, where the superstar preacher and glitzy "worship band" lift you to the heights, but in the lonely place of crushing, where God seems to be silent, prayers seem unanswered, and you hang on for dear life. "Caution! God is at work!"

C.S. Lewis observed so well that we are content with being *nice,* when all along God is intent on making us *new:*

For mere improvement is not redemption...God became man to turn creatures into sons; not simply to produce better men of the old kind but to produce a new kind of man. It is not like teaching a horse to jump better and better but like turning a horse into a winged creature.[26]

...He meant what He said. Those who put themselves in His hands will become perfect, as He is perfect—perfect in love, wisdom, joy, beauty, and immortality. The change will not be completed in this life, for death is an important part of the treatment.[27]

...Christ says "Give me All. I don't want so much of your time and so much of your money and so much of your work: I want You. I have not come to torment your natural self, but to kill it. No half-measures are any good. I don't want to cut off a branch here and a branch there, I want to have the whole tree down. I don't want to drill the tooth, or crown it, or stop it, but to have it out. Hand over the whole natural self...the whole outfit. I will give you a new self instead. In fact, I will give you Myself: my own will shall become yours.'[28]

Yoga can make you *nice* (though watch out for the demons). Therapy can make you *better*. Christ can make you *new*. When you become His possession, watch out! He won't stop until He does just that. Press into Him when He is doing His loving demolition work. Despair not. Take your refuge in Christ and His finished work on the cross for you. Feed on the precious promises for you in God's Word, and trust Him. The one who stores your tears in a bottle (Psalm 56:8) is the one who will share precious wine with you in the Kingdom of God (Matthew 26:29). (It just might be the wine is made from those same tears!)

Being confident of this, that he who began a good work in you will carry it on to completion until the day of Christ Jesus. (Philippians 1:6)

****

Beneath the Cross of Jesus

Beneath the cross of Jesus I fain would take my stand,
The shadow of a mighty rock within a weary land;
A home within the wilderness, a rest upon the way,
From the burning of the noontide heat, and the burden of the day.

O safe and happy shelter, O refuge tried and sweet,
O trysting place where Heaven's love and Heaven's justice meet!
As to the holy patriarch that wondrous dream was given,
So seems my Savior's cross to me, a ladder up to heaven.

There lies beneath its shadow but on the further side
The darkness of an awful grave that gapes both deep and wide
And there between us stands the cross two arms outstretched to save
A watchman set to guard the way from that eternal grave.

Upon that cross of Jesus mine eye at times can see
The very dying form of One Who suffered there for me;
And from my stricken heart with tears two wonders I confess;
The wonders of redeeming love and my unworthiness.

I take, O cross, thy shadow for my abiding place;
I ask no other sunshine than the sunshine of His face;
Content to let the world go by to know no gain or loss,
My sinful self my only shame, my glory all the cross.

(Elizabeth Clephane, 1830-1869)

Letter 20

Consider Him Who Is Not Fooled by Crowds

As the crowds increased, Jesus said, "This is a wicked generation." (Luke 11:29)

Friend in Jesus,

We should be eternally thankful that in many ways, Jesus is *not* like us. Things that impress us often fail to impress Jesus. Just as well, for we tend to be warped as to our values, goals, aims, and purposes. Jesus is not gullible, cannot be bribed, and is hard (impossible?) to impress (although easy to please).

> His pleasure is not in the strength of the horse, nor his delight
> in the legs of the warrior. (Psalm 147:10)

Think about crowds. Invariably we view them as a sure sign that things are going well. What can be greater proof of success than a large bunch of eager followers? Certainly big gatherings should be encouraged and never discouraged, shouldn't they? Isn't Jesus "seeker sensitive"? Well, when you even casually read the Gospel stories, you find that Jesus, during His brief days on earth, seemed to have repeated problems with crowds.

He did not seek them.
He never trusted them.
He usually lost them before the day was over.

What was His problem? Why couldn't He ease up a bit for the sake of growing His movement? I doubt many of us would hire Him as our "minister of evangelism." Consider for instance, the little episode right at the start of His ministry, recorded in John's Gospel:

> Now while he was in Jerusalem at the Passover Festival, many people saw the signs he was performing and believed in his name. But Jesus would not entrust himself to them, for he knew all people. He did not need any testimony about mankind, for he knew what was in each person. (John 2:23-25).

Did you get that? There was Jesus, at the biggest event of them all, the Passover Festival. Many people saw His signs and "believed in his name." Certainly it was time to sign them up! The young man and His fledgling movement were striking gold—in Jerusalem of all places. This opportunity, one would think, is just too good to pass up. Our modern methods would tell us to get them to belong...worry about behaviour later: "Deal with the heart later, just get them *in.*" Jesus would have none of it. He was completely unimpressed: *"But Jesus would not entrust himself to them."* He knew the *hearts* of the people and He could see that their motives were off, their goals were earthly, and they were after something different than He was offering.

He did not take their bait.
He did not commit.
He did not cash in on the moment.

He lost the crowd. By today's standards, He blew it. He did this kind of thing more than once. Think of the one we call the "rich young ruler" (Mark 10:17-31). Here was a cash cow if ever there was one. A young man of influence and power, with loads of ready money, and he wanted to join up with Jesus and His disciples. However, Jesus challenged his heart and let him go. I can imagine at least one of the disciples (Judas) being livid with carnal misunderstanding. Here was the first "big break" for the Jesus Movement, and Jesus put the guy off! He did not chase after him. He made no special provision. He lets the movement suffer the loss of a sure winner because:

> The Lord does not look at the things people look at. People look at the outward appearance, but the Lord looks at the heart. (1 Samuel 16:7)

How wonderful it is that our Lord Jesus is not swayed by earthly power, and is therefore incorruptible. He cannot be bribed. He has no price. Just think what our Christian experience would be like if Jesus had displayed even a shred of corruption. What if the Gospel narratives contained some of the dark corners found in the biographies of the very greatest of mere men...including those around whom veneration and worship have grown: Gandhi, Muhammad, John Kennedy, Dr. Martin Luther King, Jr., and others? Our hearts would be left void of the treasure we have in our impeccable Saviour. The great men and women of history are as flawed and corruptible as the rest of us...every one of us. Power and acclaim attract, and then ruin fallen people. Jesus was not drawn in by such. He rebuked the power and popularity hungry religious leaders of His day, even as He would rebuke us today:

> He said to them, "You are the ones who justify yourselves in the eyes of others, but God knows your hearts. What people value highly is detestable in God's sight." (Luke 16:15)

Let's visit one more telling scene, the so-called "triumphal entry." It was the last week of Jesus' earthly life. With His whole being firmly fixed upon His saving mission and the cross before Him, He traveled from Bethany to Jerusalem, where He was met by a cheering crowd. "Hosanna," the thousands cry, "save now!" The crowd was all for Jesus...at least a Jesus of their own manufacture. They were sure this was their moment. The King of Kings had come! "Save now!" "Hosanna!" As far as the crowd was concerned, this did not *not* mean their king would take their sins away, but take Rome away. The whole Palm Sunday scene was a tragic misunderstanding. Even those with pretty good hearts (Luke 19:37-40), had a pretty poor grasp on just what was happening. The crowd wanted a saviour from Rome, not a Saviour from sin. They wanted earthly power; Jesus wanted to save them from sin and Hell. The event that brought hysterical elation to the crowd brought sorrow to Jesus:

> As he approached Jerusalem and saw the city, he wept over it and said, "If you, even you, had only known on this day what would bring you peace—but now it is hidden from your eyes." (Luke 19:41-42)

Before the week was out, the same crowd would call for Jesus' blood.

Jesus is not a political figure. He is not one who plays to our agenda or the call of the crowds. He is the Saviour of sinners, the King over the only eternal kingdom, the Incorruptible God. His goal is not crowds, power, or popularity, but faithfulness to His Father. He sees hearts, knows secrets, and discerns motives. He is there for the humble and opposes the proud. He is unimpressed by the big, and does not overlook the insignificantly small. He is worthy of our trembling devotion, trust, and loyalty.

Bernard of Clairvaux (1091-1153) was a Catholic monk known for his deep piety and devotion to Jesus Christ. Four hundred years after he walked this earth, Martin Luther called him "the best monk that ever lived, whom I admire beyond all the rest put together." Of all of his rich writings, perhaps none has stood the test of time and blessed so many as his hymn, "O Sacred Head, Now Wounded." Most modern hymn books, if they have this hymn at all, have reduced it from its eleven verses to a weakened three or four...no doubt to suit the shrunken spiritual stature of the modern crowd. You will find all eleven below. Take your time to feast on them, because the crowd won't bother to.

****

O Sacred Head, Now Wounded

O sacred Head, now wounded, with grief and shame weighed down,
Now scornfully surrounded, with thorns Thine only crown;
O sacred Head, what glory, what bliss till now was Thine!
Yet, though despised and gory, I joy to call Thee mine.

What Thou, my Lord, hast suffered, was all for sinners' gain;
Mine, mine was the transgression, but Thine the deadly pain.
Lo, here I fall, my Savior! 'Tis I deserve Thy place;
Look on me with Thy favor, vouchsafe to me Thy grace.

Men mock and taunt and jeer Thee, Thou noble countenance,
Though mighty worlds shall fear Thee and flee before Thy glance.
How art thou pale with anguish, with sore abuse and scorn!
How doth Thy visage languish that once was bright as morn!

Now from Thy cheeks has vanished their color once so fair;
From Thy red lips is banished the splendor that was there.
Grim death, with cruel rigor, hath robbed Thee of Thy life;
Thus Thou hast lost Thy vigor, Thy strength in this sad strife.

My burden in Thy Passion, Lord, Thou hast borne for me,
For it was my transgression which brought this woe on Thee.
I cast me down before Thee, wrath were my rightful lot;
Have mercy, I implore Thee; Redeemer, spurn me not!

What language shall I borrow to thank Thee, dearest friend,
For this Thy dying sorrow, Thy pity without end?
O make me Thine forever, and should I fainting be,
Lord, let me never, never outlive my love to Thee.

My Shepherd, now receive me; my Guardian, own me Thine.
Great blessings Thou didst give me, O source of gifts divine.

Thy lips have often fed me with words of truth and love;
Thy Spirit oft hath led me to heavenly joys above.

Here I will stand beside Thee, from Thee I will not part;
O Savior, do not chide me! When breaks Thy loving heart,
When soul and body languish in death's cold, cruel grasp,
Then, in Thy deepest anguish, Thee in mine arms I'll clasp.

The joy can never be spoken, above all joys beside,
When in Thy body broken I thus with safety hide
O Lord of Life, desiring Thy glory now to see,
Beside Thy cross expiring, I'd breathe my soul to Thee.

My Savior, be Thou near me when death is at my door;
Then let Thy presence cheer me, forsake me nevermore!
When soul and body languish, oh, leave me not alone,
But take away mine anguish by virtue of Thine own!

Be Thou my consolation, my shield when I must die;
Remind me of Thy passion when my last hour draws nigh.
Mine eyes shall then behold Thee, upon Thy cross shall dwell,
My heart by faith enfolds Thee. Who dieth thus dies well.

(Bernard of Clairvaux, 1091-1153)

Letter 21

Consider Him Upon Whom the Rescued Do Lean

Who is this coming up from the wilderness leaning on her beloved? (Song of Songs 8:5)

Dear Friend in Christ,

For most of my Christian life, I left the little book *Song of Songs* largely alone. I really did not want to read about perfume and jewels! Give me wars and battles!

Over the last few years, I have come to see this love song as a wonderful picture of the relationship of Jesus with His Church...with you and me. Maybe I am getting "soft" with the passing of time, or maybe I am finally going deeper with Jesus (probably a bit of both), but I now love Song of Songs. It has helped me to consider Jesus in new ways, and has reshaped some of my ideas of Him...and ideas matter.

As Song of Songs unfolds, the lover and the loved one move through many seasons in their relationship together. The loved one (the Church) is often fickle, afraid, and hesitant. The lover (Jesus) pursues, retreats, and then wins the heart of his beloved. Near the end of the book, the watching "friends" see a beautiful sight and ask the question:

Who is this coming up from the wilderness leaning on her beloved? (Song of Songs 8:5)

Here we have a wonderful picture of the goal of our salvation: The loved one at rest in the safe and secure embrace of the Loving One. There is no more fickleness, hesitancy, running, or fear. Instead, we now see:

A Welcomed *Desperation*

A Beautiful *Dependence*

A Wonderful *Deliverance*

A Certain *Delight*

A Welcomed Desperation

For most of our lives, we run from those things which would bring us to brokenness. We fear the hard times and cling to the good times. However, there is a beauty in this picture, born of desperation. The loved one (the Church) has been in the wilderness. Times in the wilderness are lean, but not unproductive. They can bring us to a place of desperation, and once we find Jesus in a new way through that desperation, it becomes a welcome thing, for it has brought us closer to our Jesus.

A Beautiful Dependence

The proud fight for independence is over. There is a sweet surrender. Independence, which once seemed so attractive, is traded in for a beautiful dependence. Free from the drug of freedom, the loved one rests in total reliance upon the strength of the lover (Jesus). There is peace because the striving is over. The strutting has ceased; no more pretended sovereignty.

A Wonderful Deliverance

The two are as one, coming out of the wilderness. One is weary, the other strong and able, but they are coming out as one. There is a deliverance from all in the past. The tears and trials have done their work. The lover is more precious to the loved one than ever before. Out they come! Rescued, restored, and rejoicing, the lover keeps the loved one safe and secure.

A Certain Delight

What can be more delightful than these two hearts together? Finally, the loved one surrenders to the lover's care. The loved one has at last ceased all her foolishness and is in the embrace of her lover. Certain delight is in both. Salvation brings joy and delight to the Saviour as certainly as it does to the saved one.

Whatever brings us to a place of leaning upon our Saviour is, in the end, a precious thing. For one "leaner," Fanny Crosby, it was the tragedy of childhood blindness. Fanny was probably the most prolific hymnist in history. Though blinded by an incompetent doctor at six weeks of age, she wrote over 8,000 hymns. About her blindness, she wrote:

> It seemed intended by the blessed providence of God that I should be blind all my life, and I thank him for the dispensation. If perfect earthly sight were offered me tomorrow I would not accept it. I might not have sung hymns to the praise of God if I had been distracted by the beautiful and interesting things about me.[29]

It is my prayer that this will be a picture of each of us with Jesus. May our lives be marked as those who ever lean upon the one who loves us.

****

All The Way My Savior Leads Me

All the way my Savior leads me;
What have I to ask beside?
Can I doubt His tender mercy,
Who through life has been my Guide?

Heav'nly peace, divinest comfort,
Here by faith in Him to dwell!
For I know, whate'er befall me,
Jesus doeth all things well;
For I know, whate'er befall me,
Jesus doeth all things well.

All the way my Savior leads me,
Cheers each winding path I tread;
Gives me grace for every trial,
Feeds me with the living Bread.
Though my weary steps may falter,
And my soul athirst may be,
Gushing from the Rock before me,
Lo! A spring of joy I see;
Gushing from the Rock before me,
Lo! A spring of joy I see.

All the way my Savior leads me
O the fullness of His love!
Perfect rest to me is promised
In my Father's house above.
When my spirit, clothed immortal,
Wings its flight to realms of day
This my song through endless ages—
Jesus led me all the way;
This my song through endless ages—
Jesus led me all the way.

(Fanny Crosby, 1820-1915)

Letter 22

Consider Him Who Makes Us One with Himself

I am the vine; you are the branches. If you remain in me and I in you, you will bear much fruit; apart from me you can do nothing. (John 15:5)

Dear Friend in Jesus,

Imagine that you desired to be a magical guitarist, and classical guitar virtuosos Andres Segovia could somehow come and live within you... that you could somehow be in union with him. What wonders would flow from your fingers! Perhaps you desire to be an enchanted artist. Imagine Rembrandt actually dwelling within your very self. Think of what glories would flow from your heart, through the brush, and to the canvas!

The Bible presents the Christian life as supernatural. Not to be lived simply trying to imitate Jesus, the Christian life is a very real spiritual union with Jesus. This is not make-believe. The Christian does not pretend that the Spirit of Jesus Christ lives in him. Rather, he believes what Jesus says:

I will ask the Father, and he will give you another advocate to help you and be with you forever—the Spirit of truth....you know him, for he lives with you and will be in you. I will not leave you as orphans; I will come to you....On that day you will realize that I am in my Father, and you are in me, and I am in you....Anyone who loves me will obey my teaching.

My Father will love them, and we will come to them and make our home with them. (John 14:16-23)

The radical individualism of our modern world is foreign to the real world of the Bible. In the Bible, we are all joined to each other because we are connected to Jesus. We *belong* to one another and we *belong* to Jesus—not in the modern sense that one belongs to his fitness club or political party, but in a much deeper and more profound sense.

The Christian is actually spiritually united with Jesus Christ. To get the amazing truth of this union across to us, the Bible uses many wonderful pictures to describe the believer's relationship with his Saviour:

- vine and branches
- shepherd and sheep
- friend and befriended
- family

and most profoundly,

- husband and wife.

As much as Christ is in the believer, so the favourite description of a Christian in the New Testament is the simple, yet profound, "in Christ." Christ is in us, and we are in Him.

- We were "baptized into Christ Jesus." (Romans 6:3)
- We are "dead to sin but alive to God in Christ Jesus." (Romans 6:11)
- We have "eternal life in Christ Jesus our Lord." (Romans 6:23)

- There is now "no condemnation for those who are in Christ Jesus." (Romans 8:1)

- We are "sanctified in Christ Jesus." (1 Corinthians 1:2)

- We will "in Christ all...be made alive." (1 Corinthians 15:22)

- All of God's promises "are 'Yes' in Christ." (2 Corinthians 1:20)

- God has reconciled us "to himself in Christ." (2 Corinthians 5:19)

- We are "new creations in Christ." (2 Corinthians 5:17)

- We have "freedom...in Christ Jesus." (Galatians 2:4)

- We are "justified in Christ." (Galatians 2:17)

- We have "every spiritual blessing in Christ." (Ephesians 1:3)

- We are "included in Christ." (Ephesians 1:13)

- God has "raised us up with Christ and seated us with him in the heavenly realms in Christ Jesus." (Ephesians 2:6)

- We are "God's holy people in Christ Jesus." (Philippians 1:1)

- God has called us "heavenward in Christ Jesus." (Philippians 3:14)

- God guards your "hearts and your minds in Christ Jesus." (Philippians 4:7)

- We are "mature in Christ." (Colossians 1:28)

- We have "been brought to fullness in Christ." (Colossians 2:10)

- Our lives are now "hidden with Christ in God." (Colossians 2:3)

- We can "give thanks in all circumstances; for this is God's will...in Christ Jesus." (1 Thessalonians 5:18)

- We are "strong in the grace that is in Christ Jesus." (2 Timothy 2:1)

- There is "peace to all of you who are in Christ." (1 Peter 5:14)

- We are companions in the "suffering and kingdom and patient endurance...in Jesus." (Revelation 1:9)

Now, you may have read the above way too fast! Each truth is worthy of an hour or two (or perhaps a week or two) of prayerful consideration. Each is worthy of slow feasting in our fast-food world, that our souls might be truly nourished. That phrase, "in Christ," simply refers to our union with Jesus. This union is real, and it *is* the Christian life. It is not the deeper life reserved for a select few, but what God does to us—every one of us—spiritually and supernaturally, when we believe in Jesus.

Now, I don't fully grasp this. Nevertheless, I do receive it as true because God says it is true. It is not just that with Jesus, I am not alone. It is more than that. Jesus is not just with me; I am in a vital and victorious union with Him. Nowhere is this more evident than in terms of my salvation, where "God made him who had no sin to be sin for us, so that in him we might become the righteousness of God" (2 Corinthians 5:21). Our union with Christ involves a full subsuming, on His part, of all of our humanity, in *all* its fallenness, yet without sinning, and the full subsuming, on our part, of His humanity in *all* its sinlessness, even as we yet battle with sin. Mysterious? Yes. Absurd? No. Glorious? Wondrous? Awesome? Yes! Yes! Yes!

Let's take a moment and listen to John Calvin, and then to Martin Luther:

We see that our whole salvation and all its parts are comprehended in Christ. We should therefore take care not to derive the least portion of it from anywhere else. If we seek salvation, we are taught by the very name of Jesus that it is "of him." If we seek any other gifts of the Spirit, they will be found in his anointing. If we seek strength, it lies in his dominion; if purity, in his conception; if gentleness, it appears in his birth. For by his birth he was made like us in all respects that he might learn to feel our pain. If we seek redemption, it lies in his passion; if acquittal, in his condemnation; if remission of the curse, in his cross; if satisfaction, in his sacrifice; if purification, in his blood; if reconciliation, in his descent into hell; if mortification of the flesh, in his tomb; if newness of life, in his resurrection; if immortality, in the same; if inheritance of all blessings, in his Kingdom; if untroubled expectation of judgment, in the power given to him to judge. In short, since rich store of every kind of good abounds in him, let us drink our fill from this fountain, and from no other.[30]

Faith therefore must be purely taught: namely, that by faith thou art so entirely and nearly joined to Christ, that he and thou are made as it were one person; so that thou mayest boldly say: I am now one with Christ, that is to say, Christ's righteousness, victory, and life are mine. And again, Christ may say: I am that sinner, that is, his sins, death &c. are mine, because he is united and joined unto me, and I unto him. For by faith we are so joined together, that we are become one flesh and one bone…So that this faith doth couple Christ and me more near together, than the husband is couple to his wife.[31]

In the mysteries of God, we have been numbered with Jesus Christ in His death, and in His new life. Again, this is not just some sort of fiction or sleight of hand. In the mind and ways of God, it is a redemptive reality (Ideas matter to God too!):

For if we have been united with him in a death like his, we will certainly also be united with him in a resurrection like his. For we know that our old self was crucified with him so that the body ruled by sin might be done away with, that we should no longer be slaves to sin— because anyone who has died has been set free from sin.

Now if we died with Christ, we believe that we will also live with him. For we know that since Christ was raised from the dead, he cannot die again; death no longer has mastery over him. The death he died, he died to sin once for all; but the life he lives, he lives to God. (Romans 6:5-10)

As I write these words, the snow is falling on a bitterly cold Midwestern winter's day. My ancient left knee is on strike, my family is out and about, and I am about an inch away from throwing a major pity party. You may know the kind, the ones where no one comes except you. However, the *fact* is that I am in true and real union with Jesus Christ at this very moment. I don't mean that I feel His presence, because right now I don't. All I feel is a throb in my leg! What I do mean is that *God* sees me as saved, sanctified, and secure *in* His Son. This is *reality* as God sees it and therefore, needs to be reality as I see it.

I cannot come up with a better analogy for this than those God has provided, which I have shared above: vine and branches, shepherd and sheep, friend and befriended, family, and husband and wife. These everyday pictures tell me of a deeper spiritual reality. Chew on them. The Christian's life is not like the life of the unbeliever, because Jesus is in the believer, and the believer is in Christ. It is in this union that we love, live, battle, die, and rise again. The living, loving, conquering, dying, rising one lives in us, really, and we live in Him.

Apart from this reality, we have nothing. Because of this reality, we have all things.

My beloved is mine and I am his. (Song of Songs 2:16)

****

A Wonderful Savior Is Jesus My Lord

A wonderful Savior is Jesus my Lord,
A wonderful Savior to me;
He hideth my soul in the cleft of the rock,
Where rivers of pleasure I see.

He hideth my soul in the cleft of the rock,
That shadows a dry, thirsty land;
He hideth my life in the depths of His love,
And covers me there with His hand,
And covers me there with His hand.

A wonderful Savior is Jesus my Lord,
He taketh my burden away,
He holdeth me up and I shall not be moved,
He giveth me strength as my day.

With numberless blessings each moment He crowns,
And filled with His fullness divine,
I sing in my rapture, oh, glory to God!
For such a Redeemer as mine.

When clothed with His brightness transported I rise
To meet Him in clouds of the sky,
His perfect salvation, His wonderful love,
I'll shout with the millions on high.

He hideth my soul in the cleft of the rock,
That shadows a dry, thirsty land;
He hideth my life in the depths of His love,
And covers me there with His hand,
And covers me there with His hand.

(Fanny Crosby, 1820-1915)

Letter 23

Consider Him Who Gives Courage to Cowards

When they saw the courage of Peter and John and realized that they were unschooled, ordinary men, they were aston-ished and they took note that these men had been with Jesus.
(Acts 4:13)

Dear Fellow Follower,

A small metal cross on a cobbled portion of Broad Street, Oxford, marks the very spot where, on October 16, 1555, Hugh Latimer, the Bishop of Worcester, and Nicholas Ridley, the Bishop of London, were burned at the stake together. Their crime? Simply believing and teaching that a person is made right before God by faith in Christ alone, without the interference of pope, priest, or mass.

All they had to do in order to accommodate Mary I, Queen of England, and thus avoid death, was keep quiet about the Gospel.

Not a chance!

Ridley's death was particularly horrific, as the flames burned poorly and consumed his lower body, but not his upper body, leaving him conscious and in torment for a long time. While the flames went about their terrible business, Hugh Latimer is purported to have said these timeless words to his companion in suffering:

> Be of good cheer, Ridley; and play the man. We shall this day, by God's grace, light up such a candle in England, as I trust, will never be put out.[32]

147

It is worth asking: "Where do people get such courage…courage to live by steadfast convictions rather than passing interests…courage to stand upon the Gospel no matter what it may cost them?"

By comparison to Ridley and Latimer, we are a generation of cowards. We readily give up. Our feelings are easily hurt. We quickly run away when we should hold our ground. We let go of convictions in order to preserve our comforts. Most of us have had such soft lives, so free from conflict, that when difficulties come our way and moral, financial, vocational, or relational challenges confront us, we cave in. We quit our marriages, desert our posts, and go AWOL on our families, communities, and ministries. We lack the "stuff" it takes to hang in there, to see things through, and to fight on.

We are a generation of quitters. There…I said it. We are akin to Groucho Marx, who quipped:

"Those are my principles! And, if you don't like them…well…
I have others."

However, I feel I must cut deeper. These are days that demand what we are not. We are quitters in an age that needs stayers. We are cowards in an age that needs us to be courageous. The call is for brave men and women. The need of the hour is for soldiers who will not leave their posts. We need husbands, fathers, wives, mothers, grandparents, and young people who will rather die right than live wrong; who will keep their promises even when it becomes costly; who will live for Jesus and His kingdom even when every pressure is on them to cut their losses and run. We need men for whom ideas matter, whose thinking has been shaped by the Bible and who, in considering the worth of Christ, have concluded that He is to be treasured above all passing comforts and interests.

The times are calling for a generation of bold souls like our fathers, but they are stuck with us. So is God. We are all He has.

If things were up to us, the future would be pretty bleak. I can imagine society collapsing around us while the "men" of our generation play their computer games. However, I do not have to imagine it. I am experiencing it.

Thankfully, it is not all up to us. Bring Jesus and His Holy Spirit into the picture and everything changes. Jesus gives courage to cowards and turns the hapless into heroes—He really does.

Let's explore.

Whatever else the book of the Acts is, it is certainly a story of how Jesus makes people brave. The raw material—the men and women who followed Jesus at the birth of the Church—were not exactly an impressive lot. We find locked doors, hiding men, Christ-denying, fearful, flinching, failing followers. Not exactly the kind of people you need to change the world. However, all through Acts, the Holy Spirit empowered those men and women of the Church of Jesus to be bold. (Although often called "The Acts of the Apostles", it might better be called "Acts of the Holy Spirit"). Read it yourself. Insert yourself into it. Get down on the floor and pound it, believing and begging God to make *you* a brave soul for these needy days, as He did *them* for their needy days.

Just look at a few inspiring examples below.

Peter on Pentecost

Then Peter stood up with the Eleven, raised his voice and addressed the crowd: "Fellow Jews and all of you who live in Jerusalem, let me explain this to you; listen carefully to what I say."...With many other words he warned them; and he pleaded with them, "Save yourselves from this corrupt generation." (Acts 2:14, 40, though see Acts 2:14-40 for the entire account)

Peter to the Rulers of Israel

Then Peter, filled with the Holy Spirit, said to them: "Rulers and elders of the people! If we are being called to account today for an act of kindness shown to a man who was lame and are being asked how he was healed, then know this, you and all the people of Israel: It is by the name of Jesus Christ of Nazareth, whom you crucified but whom God raised from the dead, that this man stands before you healed. Jesus is

> "'the stone you builders rejected,
> which has become the cornerstone.'

Salvation is found in no one else, for there is no other name under heaven given to mankind by which we must be saved."... Then they called them in again and commanded them not to speak or teach at all in the name of Jesus. But Peter and John replied, "Which is right in God's eyes: to listen to you, or to him? You be the judges!" (Acts 4:8-12, 18- 19)

Stephen Before the Sanhedrin

"You stiff-necked people! Your hearts and ears are still uncircumcised. You are just like your ancestors: You always resist the Holy Spirit! Was there ever a prophet your ancestors did not persecute? They even killed those who predicted the coming of the Righteous One. And now you have betrayed and murdered him—you who have received the law that was given through angels but have not obeyed it." (Acts 7:51-53)

Paul Before the Sanhedrin

Paul looked straight at the Sanhedrin and said, "My brothers, I have fulfilled my duty to God in all good conscience to this day." At this the high priest Ananias ordered those standing near Paul to strike him on the mouth. Then Paul said to him, "God will strike you, you whitewashed wall! You sit there to judge me according to the law, yet you yourself violate the law by commanding that I be struck!" (Acts 23:1-3)

Scorching Stuff!

Examples from the Bible could fill a book: Daniel, Philip, Esther, Elijah, and many more. Examples from Christian history could fill a library: Polycarp, Justin Martyr, Judson, Taylor, Wesley, Wurmbrand, and countless others. The evidence is in, and the results are clear:

Jesus Christ Makes People Brave

So, where does this leave us? There is no cavalry coming over the hill to rescue us in our situation. There is no point in looking to someone to do our job for us. We need to face reality. Though we are soft and selfish, the need of the day is for men and women who are ready to live...and die...for the treasure we call the Gospel. However, *Jesus* will make us courageous. He really will. Yet we need to want it. We need to get to a place where we say, "Enough!" to triumphs of darkness in our day and to our cowardly love of ease and comfort. I just checked, and this verse is still in the Bible:

For the eyes of the Lord range throughout the earth to strengthen those whose hearts are fully committed to him. (2 Chronicles 16:9)

I am so glad that the story of Nate Saint, Jim Elliot, Ed McCully, Pete Fleming, and Roger Youderian came my way a few decades ago in the form of Elizabeth Elliot's book, *Through Gates of Splendor.* How the story of those five brave young men stirred my young heart! It stirs it still!

On January 7, 1956, the night before those men ventured to take the Gospel to the Auca Indians of Ecuador, they commended themselves and their young wives and families to the God who had given them courage and heart. They sang the hymn I share with you below. The next day, a Gospel work was begun amongst those Indians...at the cost of the lives of these five...*brave*...young men.

****

We Rest on Thee, Our Shield and Our Defender!

We rest on Thee, our Shield and our Defender!
We go not forth alone against the foe;
Strong in Thy strength, safe in Thy keeping tender,
We rest on Thee, and in Thy Name we go.
Strong in Thy strength, safe in Thy keeping tender,
We rest on Thee, and in Thy Name we go.

Yes, in Thy Name, O Captain of salvation!
In Thy dear Name, all other names above;
Jesus our Righteousness, our sure Foundation,
Our Prince of glory and our King of love.
Jesus our Righteousness, our sure Foundation,
Our Prince of glory and our King of love.

We go in faith, our own great weakness feeling,
And needing more each day Thy grace to know:
Yet from our hearts a song of triumph pealing,
"We rest on Thee, and in Thy Name we go."
Yet from our hearts a song of triumph pealing,
"We rest on Thee, and in Thy Name we go."

We rest on Thee, our Shield and our Defender!
Thine is the battle, Thine shall be the praise;
When passing through the gates of pearly splendor,
Victors, we rest with Thee, through endless days.
When passing through the gates of pearly splendor,
Victors, we rest with Thee, through endless days.

(Edith Cherry, 1872-1897)[33]

(You will see that Edith Cherry lived to the ripe old age of 25. She wrote two full volumes of hymns!)

Letter 24

Consider Him Who Alone Can Define Marriage

*"Haven't you read," he replied, "that at the beginning the
Creator 'made them male and female,' and said, 'For this
reason a man will leave his father and mother and be united
to his wife, and the two will become one flesh'? So they are
no longer two, but one flesh. Therefore what God has joined
together, let no one separate,"* (Matthew 19:4-6)

Dear Clear Thinker,

If you want to know the nature and purpose of a thing, do not ask
the thing. Things cannot define themselves. Nor can they define other
things, at least not very well. You must go beyond the thing, outside
of it, and ask its creator if you are to get a clear picture of the nature
and purpose of the created thing. The maker alone really understands
it. Only the artist really understands what he means to convey through
his masterpiece. Only the craftsman fully understands the purpose and
value of the object crafted.

The Bible plainly teaches us that Jesus is the maker of all that
there is. He has made all things.

> Through him all things were made; without him nothing was
> made that has been made. (John 1:3)

> For in him all things were created: things in heaven and on
> earth, visible and invisible, whether thrones or powers or

rulers or authorities; all things have been created through him and for him. (Colossians 1:16)

Now, to be overly obvious: Since Jesus made all things, He made man and woman as well. Men are things, women are things. The Bible tells us that He made marriage, and marriage is a thing. Since only the maker of a thing really understands the thing, only God—Jesus Christ—can define marriage in any proper way. The Christian, at least the consistent Christian, can conclude nothing else.

Today, our culture is confused about marriage for a very simple... and wicked...reason: It does not want the maker of marriage to set the definition for marriage. It does not like the maker of marriage. People (things) want to define marriage (another thing) without any reference to Jesus Christ (the maker of both "things").

This is absurd and impossible, rebellious and wicked.

Jesus is very clear in His definition of marriage. There is absolutely nothing vague about this. Jesus is not confused. He clearly tells us four simple, unmistakable *truths* about marriage. These are so plain that they would make our confusion laughable, except for the fact that our confusion is born in our deliberate rebellion against God. It is anything but funny.

Marriage is:

- God's creation and God's idea. Therefore, it does not owe its origin or definition to shifting society and is not susceptible to the changing winds and whims of sinful cultures.

- Between a man and a woman. This is what Jesus says. A man cannot marry another man, nor a woman another woman. It does not matter what you or I think about this. We did not invent marriage, so we cannot define it.

- A mystical union where two become one.

- A public and permanent covenant made in front of and by God. God joins the man and woman together, and we do not have the authority to undo the union God makes.

These things are so clear as to leave no room for debate.

Let's focus on the profound reference to the two becoming one flesh. This is remarkably holy and speaks of the sexual union between a husband and wife. The apostle Paul tells us that the marriage of a man and a woman is to be a "picture" of the mystery of the union of Jesus and His Bride, the Church:

> "For this reason a man will leave his father and mother and be united to his wife, and the two will become one flesh." This is a profound mystery—but I am talking about Christ and the church. (Ephesians 5:31-33)

Here is why sexuality and marriage are and must remain very sacred. They are symbols, pictures, of the covenant and union Jesus has with us. Of course, Jesus' union with us is *not* sexual, but the intimacy of the marital sexual union is intended by God to be a picture—the closest picture possible—of our relationship with our Saviour. Therefore, to take sexuality and remove it from its deepest intended purpose and place it in *any* other sphere is the gravest of sins.

I know it is commonly said that "all sins are the same," but does the Bible teach this? True, all sins are an offense to God. True, all sins separate us from God. However, some sins are certainly more grievous due to the image they deface, and their consequences—social, spiritual, and relational. Sexual sin, it would reasonably seem, is especially grave as it defaces the image of Christ and His Church, and produces no end of social, spiritual, and relational troubles.

According to the definition provided by the designer, Jesus, the union of husband and wife, when most intimately experienced, is *intended* to be a pure and beautiful representation of the covenant love Jesus has for His Bride.

We see here the deep spiritual tragedy of fornication, adultery, self-abuse, homosexual behaviour, and divorce.

By the way, I once heard a good man, a minister of the Gospel, teach that the primary purpose of marital sex was to make children. I know this is why animals have sex (presumably the *only* reason animals have sex). Certainly this good man was mistaken. Certainly he reduced the marital union from its intended glory to the realm of the beasts. Certainly the marital union, at its purest, is to reflect like nothing else can, the love, joy, acceptance, permanence, exclusivity, and security that the Church has with its Saviour.

You cannot just throw a tantrum and make marriage what you want it to be because it suits you. Neither can I. For a man to live with a woman out of wedlock as though they were married is to offend God, society, and each other. For two men (or women) to get "married" is by definition impossible. To fornicate is, as C.S. Lewis said, like chewing food and then spitting it out.

True believers in Jesus need to get back to clear, plain thinking and speaking in this matter of marriage. Somebody (the Church!) needs to step up and declare that the emperor has no clothes on. Someone needs to have the courage to state the obvious and pay the price for it. Anything less on our part is unfaithfulness to God and to our culture—a culture to which we are called to be loving prophets, not politicians.

In the end, this whole discussion and the confusion which surrounds it is founded in and fueled by a rebellious spirit which refuses to honour Jesus Christ, the maker of all things. The only way out of this mess is repentance, and a return in and through Jesus Christ. The hymn below is rare for its reverence, but only in such reverence is the remedy for our times found.

****

Praise, My Soul, the King of Heaven

> Praise, my soul, the King of heaven;
> To His feet thy tribute bring.
> Ransomed, healed, restored, forgiven,
> Evermore His praises sing:
> Alleluia! Alleluia!
> Praise the everlasting King.

Praise Him for His grace and favour
To our fathers in distress.
Praise Him still the same as ever,
Slow to chide, and swift to bless.
Alleluia! Alleluia!
Glorious in His faithfulness.

Frail as summer's flower we flourish,
Blows the wind and it is gone;
But while mortals rise and perish
Our God lives unchanging on,
Praise Him, Praise Him, Hallelujah
Praise the High Eternal One!

Fatherlike He tends and spares us;
Well our feeble frame He knows.
In His hands He gently bears us,
Rescues us from all our foes.
Alleluia! Alleluia!
Widely yet His mercy flows.

Angels, help us to adore Him;
Ye behold Him face to face;
Sun and moon, bow down before Him,
Dwellers all in time and space.
Alleluia! Alleluia!
Praise with us the God of grace.

(Henry Francis Lyte, 1793-1847)

Letter 25

Consider Him Whose Grace Makes One Tremble

If you, Lord, kept a record of sin, Lord, who could stand? But with you there is forgiveness, so that we can, with reverence, serve you. (Psalm 130:3-4)

Dear Trembler,

More often than not, grace is misunderstood. Grace is *not* God saying, in regard to our sin:

"That's O.K."

"Just forget it."

"It really does not matter."

When understood rightly, grace is the most unexpected, undeserved, astounding, breathtaking, tremble-producing gift in the universe. Grace is not God shrugging His shoulders and, with a chuckle, and letting us off the hook.

Grace resulted in a bleeding Son on a lonely hill. Grace is the way a white-hot, holy God has designed to be both just and the justifier of sinners. Grace is worthy of the word, "awesome."

There are two words in Psalm 130:4 which must always be found together. Do you see them? I am speaking of *forgiveness* and *reverence. Forgiveness* is the *reverence producing* way that God deals with our sins through the Gospel.

The King James Version (KJV) translates this verse this way:

But there is forgiveness with thee, that thou mayest be feared.

The New English Translation (NET) gives us:

But you are willing to forgive, so that you might be honored.

And the Good News Translation (GNT):

But you forgive us, so that we should stand in awe of you.

"Feared," "honored," "stand in awe of." This is what *forgiveness*, properly understood, *must* produce.

However, when misunderstood, the amazing forgiveness of God as seen in the Gospel, is taken with a complacent yawn. Seeing God as being basically like us, only a bit bigger, we view forgiveness almost as a right, what God *ought* to give us or had better give us—what we somehow deserve. Such bad thinking cheapens the Gospel, cheapens grace, and cheapens forgiveness. No one will live and die for a cheap imitation. Ideas matter.

No! May it never be! We ought to tremble and revere, be awe-struck and fear—*not* because we are damned (for the damned will tremble and fear and be awestruck too, but in a very different way), but because we are not! We ought to be in jaw-dropping wonder because our sin-hating God has had mercy upon us through Christ. For the redeemed, there can be no other proper response.

Trembling? Awe? Fear? Honour? These are what the Gospel produces in the reverent soul. Has it produced such in yours?

Imagine a holy God who owes us nothing, but who, from the depths of His heart, righteously designs to deal with our sin in mercy. This God predestines, calls, justifies, and glorifies miserable offenders like us. He invites, forgives, preserves, and embraces, securing multitudes—you and me included. He delivers us together from a deserved Hell unto a glorious Heaven—all through the Gospel.

And we don't tremble?

No, we *don't* tremble.

The reality of the tremble-producing Gospel began to grip me when I started wrestling with Dietrich Bonhoeffer's writing. The truths he presented to my young heart pinned me to the mat in surrender. His words (especially those below) began to revolutionize my mind—a mind that had been dulled by a culture of cheap grace. It began to be sharpened by the words of one who understood the wonders of Gospel forgiveness. Don't rush through these words, but, better still, get his volcanic volume, *The Cost of Discipleship* and live in it for a month or two:

Cheap grace is the preaching of forgiveness without requiring repentance, baptism without church discipline, Communion without confession, absolution without personal confession. Cheap grace is grace without discipleship, grace without the cross, grace without Jesus Christ, living and incarnate.

Costly grace is the treasure hidden in the field; for the sake of it a man will go and sell all that he has. It is the pearl of great price to buy [for] which the merchant will sell all his goods. It is the kingly rule of Christ, for whose sake a man will pluck out the eye which causes him to stumble; it is the call of Jesus Christ at which the disciple leaves his nets and follows him.

Such grace is costly because it calls us to follow, and it is grace because it calls us to follow Jesus Christ. It is costly because it costs a man his life, and it is grace because it gives a man the only true life. It is costly because it condemns sin, and grace because it justifies the sinner. Above all, it is costly because it cost God the life of his Son: "ye were bought at a price," and what has cost God much cannot be cheap for us. Above all, it is grace because God did not reckon his Son too dear a price to pay for our life, but delivered him up for us. Costly grace is the Incarnation of God.[34]

What is the remedy for the complacent Christian? What is the remedy for *us*? How can we move from being a company of yawners with wandering minds to being a church of wonder-filled worshippers? How do we rouse our sleepy selves? I do not have an easy answer for our easy answer age. Getting a reverent heart is not as easy as opening a box and adding water. I think the only advice I have is that we fall on our faces before Heaven and plead with God to forgive our flippant, false faith, and give us the *real* faith, which properly, joyfully and reverently trembles before Him.

I offer the following Scriptures to help move your heart:

For it is written: "Be holy, because I am holy."
Since you call on a Father who judges each person's work impartially, live out your time as foreigners here in reverent fear. (1 Peter 1:16-17)

Therefore, you kings, be wise;
be warned, you rulers of the earth.
Serve the Lord with fear
and celebrate his rule with trembling.
Kiss his son, or he will be angry
and your way will lead to your destruction,
for his wrath can flare up in a moment.
Blessed are all who take refuge in him. (Psalm 2:10-12)

For all those things hath mine hand made, and all those things have been, saith the Lord: but to this man will I look, even to him that is poor and of a contrite spirit, and trembleth at my word. (Isaiah 66:2, KJV)

My flesh trembleth for fear of thee; and I am afraid of thy judgments. (Psalm 119:120, KJV)

And ye shall seek me, and find me, when ye shall search for me with all your heart. (Jeremiah 29:13, KJV)

Ask, and it shall be given you; seek, and ye shall find; knock, and it shall be opened unto you. (Matthew 7:7, KJV)

Charles Wesley was no lightweight with God. He was not a spiritual snorkeler, but a deep diver. He *knew the Lord* both in doctrine and experience. From such a trembling heart and mind came 8,898 hymns...ten lines of verse every day for fifty years.[35] Oh, for a generation of such men and women today; God saturated, reverent, on fire, world changers! He never ceased to *marvel* at the wonders of the God who saved him by His Gospel, evidenced by the all but forgotten great hymn below, thought by many to be his conversion hymn. Who writes words like these today? Who thinks such thoughts about God? Where are men and women who "rejoice with trembling" in our age? For sure, God's grace is not lacking! Believe that God can, wants to, and will give you—even you—a trembling, awestruck heart!

****

Where Shall My Wondering Soul Begin?

Where shall my wondering soul begin?
How shall I all to heaven aspire?
A slave redeemed from death and sin,
A brand plucked from eternal fire,
How shall I equal triumphs raise,
Or sing my great Deliverer's praise?

O how shall I the goodness tell,
Father, which Thou to me hast showed?
That I, a child of wrath and hell,
I should be called a child of God,

Should know, should feel my sins forgiven,
Blessed with this antepast of Heaven!

And shall I slight my Father's love?
Or basely fear His gifts to own?
Unmindful of His favors prove?
Shall I, the hallowed cross to shun,
Refuse His righteousness to impart,
By hiding it within my heart?

No! though the ancient dragon rage,
And call forth all his host to war,
Though earth's self-righteous sons engage
Them and their god alike I dare;
Jesus, the sinner's friend, proclaim;
Jesus, to sinners still the same.

Outcasts of men, to you I call,
Harlots, and publicans, and thieves!
He spreads His arms to embrace you all;
Sinners alone His grace receives;
No need of Him the righteous have;
He came the lost to seek and save.

Come, O my guilty brethren, come,
Groaning beneath your load of sin,
His bleeding heart shall make you room,
His open side shall take you in;
He calls you now, invites you home;
Come, O my guilty brethren, come!

For you the purple current flowed
In pardons from His wounded side,
Languished for you the eternal God,
For you the Prince of glory died:
Believe, and all your sin's forgiven;
Only believe, and yours is Heaven!

(Charles Wesley, 1707-1788)

Letter 26

Consider Him Who In Mercy Gives You Your Next Breath[36]

But unless you repent, you too will all perish. (Luke 13:3)

Beloved,

Which of us remains unmoved by events such as the Japanese tsunami of 2011? How our hearts broke for the thousands upon thousands of lives which were irrevocably transformed by the cataclysm which befell that country!

I feel a pastoral need to help believers reflect upon such events, for such tragic, inexplicable occurrences (what insurance companies call "acts of God") are not going to go away. Indeed, if anything, Jesus tells us we can expect them to increase.

"There will be great earthquakes, famines and pestilences in various places, and fearful events and great signs from heaven." (Luke 21:11)

An event of similar type, though not magnitude, happened in Jerusalem in Jesus' day. It "made the news," and apparently all Jerusalem was aware of it. A tower at Siloam, a place within Jerusalem, had collapsed. Eighteen people were killed when it fell. Knowing the popular mind on the event (in a "theological" sense), Jesus poses a question to the crowd before Him:

"Those eighteen who died when the tower in Siloam fell on them—do you think they were more guilty than all the others living in Jerusalem? I tell you, no! But unless you repent, you too will all perish." (Luke 13:4-5)

Think about the question Jesus asks. From this question, we can clearly deduce that the common (mis)understanding of people in Jerusalem was that the eighteen who died were especially bad sinners, and therefore deserved to die, while the rest of them were, by implication, comparatively righteous and therefore safe from such judgment. This type of thinking was along the same lines as Job's friends who automatically assumed that Job's sufferings were the direct result of some form of sin in his life...a sin of which they were obviously innocent, as they were not suffering.

Now, the Lord Jesus did not fall into this theological quicksand. Had He been as biblically illiterate as His hearers, He would have succumbed to the pop theology of His day and said:

"You are right. They were worse than you. You are better than they. They got what they deserved."

However, He did not say this because He knew this wasn't true. Ideas matter to Jesus.

What He did say was devastating. In effect, His words had the force of a theological earthquake, and we need to feel the tremors of them today:

"I tell you, no! But unless you repent, you too will all perish."

Jesus' perfect, divine insight into this event was and is shocking to the
popular mind. It was shocking, no doubt, to His contemporaries, who, like us, did not know their Bibles. Biblical illiteracy is behind most all confusion and foolish thinking.

The key here is that Jesus assumed no righteousness whatsoever in any of His hearers. So, in loving concern for their souls, He warned them that they were in as great danger as those who had perished. He told them plainly that the only hope for them was to heed the warning of the disaster and get right with God. His warning to "repent" or likewise "perish" tells us that He believed:

1. The tower disaster was a judgment.

2. All people (not just those who died in the tower disaster) deserved such judgment.

3. The fact that His hearers had not yet been so judged in no way implied that they possessed superior righteousness.

4. The eighteen had "perished", and His audience was also in immediate danger of "perishing." In the language of the New Testament, "perish" refers to not just physical death, but also eternal judgment in Hell.

5. Every human being exists moment by moment by sheer mercy alone. Though deserving of judgment from the hand of a holy God at any time, we are spared a thousand times by a merciful God who wills our repentance.

6. An unobliged God mercifully invites us sinners to repent in a sure hope of mercy.

Consider a modern question the Lord Jesus did not entertain. The narrative in Luke reveals that the following question was not even in His mind, or in the minds of His hearers. Almost without exception, when such an event happens today, our generation reacts with the question:

"If God is good, how can He cause, or allow, such suffering to happen to innocent people?"

However, this modern question is flawed from the start, for it assumes the innocence of people. The Bible will not let us do so. It insists upon the indefensible guilt of the human race, the entirety of Adam's family (see Romans 3 and 5). We have to hold our minds and hearts to the Bible at times such as this, and in our genuine and proper love for our suffering fellow man, not allow ourselves to adopt the unbiblical (and therefore inept and unloving) pop theology of our day.

Notice with me that:

1. Ancient people believed in the guilt of people (even if it was other people, and not them), and therefore did not question the righteousness or wisdom of God in His judgments.

2. Modern people believe in the innocence of people, and therefore assert the unrighteousness of God in His judgments, or His impotence in not stopping all disasters, or both.

Jesus never questioned the goodness of His Heavenly Father when the tower fell. He understood that the Scriptures plainly teach that life is at best vaporous, and that all humanity exists moment by moment by the pure, undeserved mercy of God. He, the very Author of Life, knew that all His Father had to do was utter three words and a human life was ended:

"Return to dust." (Psalm 90:3)

Jesus understands that the breath I draw, I draw only by the very mercy of God. I had better understand this, too. I had also better understand that when my all-wise, Heavenly Father says to me, "Return to dust, John Gillespie," my soul had better be ready—solely by faith in the merits of Jesus who died for my sins—to see Him and give a worthy account of itself.

Ancient biblically illiterate people would have assumed that our Japanese contemporaries who suffered and died in the tsunami were wicked and got what they deserved, they themselves being righteous.

Modern biblically illiterate people will assume that the Japanese are as innocent as they, and that God (if He even exists) is either not very powerful or not very good.

Jesus teaches that all of us are equally wicked and had better repent.

So, how do we respond to a disaster such as the one which befell Japan? In light of Jesus' teaching in Luke 13, I offer the following:

1. Move in heartfelt acts of mercy for our stricken neighbours, because they are no more unrighteous than we. We all share the same human predicament and all exist by mercy alone. When God says to any of our fellows, "Return to dust," we who share this same dust have no option but to have compassion on our fellows.

2. Put our hands over our mouths and be silent before a holy God who owes us nothing but gives us life and breath (Job 4:3-5).

3. Repent as we consider the reality that in the sovereignty of God, our days are brief and His judgments are sure. In love, He warns us to turn to Him in the hope of His mercy, which He offers to a wicked race through Jesus Christ.

4. In turning to God through Jesus for mercy, be ready to be summoned at any time, at any age, to surrender your soul back to God, and, being called to your account, enter in to true life by His redeeming grace alone.

5. In gratitude for the countless mercies of Christ, urge our fellow fallen neighbours to believe on Him who alone can save them from a deserved wrath and keep them unto eternal life.

Fellow frail creature of dust, I offer these considerations in the light of the Scriptures, in the fear of God, in deepest gratitude for the grace of God which has saved me from deserved wrath, and in a spirit of love for our fallen race.

****

Father, I Stretch My Hands to Thee

Father, I stretch my hands to Thee,
No other help I know;
If Thou withdraw Thyself from me,
Ah! whither shall I go?

What did Thine only Son endure,
Before I drew my breath!
What pain, what labor, to secure
My soul from endless death!

O Jesus, could I this believe,
I now should feel Thy power;
Now my poor soul Thou wouldst retrieve,
Nor let me wait one hour.

Surely Thou canst not let me die;
O speak, and I shall live;
And here I will unwearied lie,
Till Thou Thy Spirit give.

Author of faith! to Thee I lift
My weary, longing eyes:
O let me now receive that gift!
My soul without it dies.

The worst of sinners would rejoice,
Could they but see Thy face:
O, let me hear Thy quickening voice,
And taste Thy pardoning grace.

(Charles Wesley, 1717-1788)

Letter 27

Consider Him Whose Ways with Us Are Sometimes Wrapped in Mystery

Therefore, in order to keep me from becoming conceited,
I was given a thorn in my flesh, a messenger of Satan, to
torment me. (2 Corinthians 12:7)

Dear Friend in Christ,

This letter is an attempt on my part to stimulate us toward thinking biblically about the tough issue of pain and suffering among the children of God. It is by no means exhaustive, nor does it claim to plumb the mysteries of issues surrounding God's providence or His sovereignty, and Satan's activity. While certainly in this life (and perhaps even in eternity), we may never fully understand the ways of God among us, it is my hope that we will nevertheless come ever closer to a place where we rest in the arms of our Saviour in all things and at all times, even while in the midst of a battle with the enemy of our souls!

I offer what follows in a spirit of concern for the well-being of our souls, and with a good bit of trembling as we tread softly upon such mysteries.

Consider the question:

Does God ever send sickness and calamity to His children?

Once, when preaching at a Bible conference, I made the following remark in reference to a fellow believer: "God gave him cancer and he died." That statement provoked a good amount of discussion and some consternation!

Given that I was a bit "lathered up" in the pulpit, and now in the comparatively "cooler" environment of my study, I want to try to develop not just that statement, but the thinking behind it. I wish here for us to try to think biblically, and not just move from our emotions, from "folk religion"—or worse still—from the heretical theology of some TV preachers (typically American), who promise us endless health and wealth.

In seeking a Bible-sourced answer to the question, "Does God ever send sickness and calamity to His children?", I first need to pose another question: "Were there any instances in the Bible when God actually sent sickness or calamity to His children?" If so, I need to ask a related question: "What was the purpose behind such a God-sent affliction?"

Well, even a cursory reading of the Bible will reveal numerous instances when God declared Himself to be the author of a trial, affliction, or illness visited upon one He loved. I will point out only three of many such instances.

King Uzziah (2 Chronicles 26)

King Uzziah was a good, godly, wise king of Israel. He reigned for fifty-two years. Late in his life, the Bible says he became proud and arrogant. The Word of God tells us plainly that "the Lord had afflicted him" with leprosy (2 Chronicles 26:20). The purpose? Evidently, to humble him, to preserve his soul from the radioactive sin of pride, and to preserve Israel from the horrors of an arrogant leader. It was a severe mercy on God's part.

What can we deduce from this instance? Well, we must not conclude that all illness is discipline or judgment! However, we can deduce that in a given case, an illness or trial may be an expression of discipline from the Lord, sent because God really loves His people and is more concerned for their long-term good than for their present comfort.

The Apostle Paul (2 Corinthians 12)

The apostle had been blessed with an unusual experience of the Lord. In some sense, he was caught up into the very presence of God. However, God did not want him to become spiritually proud. (God did not want him to end up like Uzziah!) Paul makes it very clear that God was behind an affliction (a "thorn in the flesh" we can presume to be a bodily trouble because of the word, "flesh"). In this case, Paul tells us that God used Satan as His instrument, but it is clear from the context that behind the "thorn" was the loving hand of God Himself. The purpose? To keep Paul reliant upon God's sufficient grace and close to Jesus, and to preserve him from the deadly sin of pride.

What can we conclude here? God may, if He deems it necessary, afflict a dear child of His, even using Satan as His "rod." He does this for the greater good of preserving his soul from the calamity of sin. God valued the health of Paul's soul above the comfort of his body.

Jesus Christ (Isaiah 53)

The prophet Isaiah summarizes the life of Christ (700 years previous to it) by telling us that God the Father was "pleased" to bruise and crush His very own beloved Son. This is not sadistic pleasure, but what the prophet is saying is that the transference of God's righteous wrath from us to Jesus "pleased" the just, redemptive plans of a holy God. The purpose? To secure a greater good in magnifying God's grace through the redemption of countless ruined sinners.

What can we conclude here? If God was willing to afflict His own Son to secure our salvation, He clearly shows that over and above physical comfort and ease (even that of His own Son), He values our deliverance from sin and securing His own glory in redeeming us. I think we can further deduce here that if a follower of Jesus needs to suffer to further the spread of the Gospel (e.g. a hospitalized Christian telling a fellow sufferer about Jesus), that God may ordain such.

These are just three instances. We could mention others: Job, Israel in the wilderness, Joseph, and many more. However, what I think we have done so far is answer the important question: "Are there any instances in the Bible of God sending sickness or calamity to His children?" By making ourselves think biblically, we have seen that the answer is plainly, "Yes." Also, in answer to the question: "What were the purposes behind such God-sent afflictions?", we have seen that God may discipline, protect from grave sin, or promote the Gospel, all through the sickness or suffering of one He loves.

(Notice what we have not said. We have not made any sweeping statements declaring that every trial or tribulation is the result of sin, lack of faith, or God's judgment.)

Having done our biblical thinking so far, here are four possible positions one can take in the case of an illness or calamity. I think two of these are biblically "in bounds," though they still leave us with questions, mysteries, and the need to simply trust the Lord in the midst of things too deep for us. I think two of these are biblically "out of bounds," and leave us truly out on the sea of despair.

Two "Out of Bounds" Options

1) A big, strong Satan overcomes the purposes of God and trumps Him in afflicting one of God's children. While this may seem to get God off the hook, it really just puts Him on a bigger one. We end up with a worldview classically called "dualism." That is, there is a war raging between a good God and an equally powerful, bad Devil. Many Christians who don't read their Bibles have unwittingly adopted the dualistic view, where a big Devil seems to get the upper hand in no end of situations. The pastoral implications of believing in a God who sometimes cannot keep up with Satan are more troublesome than those which arise from believing that a good, sovereign God may sometimes find it best to send trials to His beloved children.

The ancient book of Job tells us that Satan has no sovereign power at all, only permitted power (Job 1:6-12). The Bible teaches us that while Satan is bigger than we are, and that we must watch, pray, and be careful of him, he is infinitesimally small compared to God. Yes, we are in the midst of a genuine spiritual battle; one which can only be won through the power of the Gospel. And yes, Satan wages real war against the Church. But we cannot move from this to the dangerous mistake of believing in a big, sovereign Devil who stands as a worthy opponent to God.

2) A particular trial "just happened." Somehow, God missed one on His radar, and so a calamity befell us. Again, far from absolving God, it implicates Him. Here we have a God who befuddles, sleeps, or is caught off guard. He is really like us…Think of Morgan Freeman in the film *Bruce Almighty*. He really does His best, but He does not perfectly know the future, and sometimes just plain cannot keep up. This "God" may work in quaint Hollywood films, but is certainly not Israel's God who "neither slumbers nor sleeps" (Psalm 121:4).

Give me any day a sovereign God who, for reasons I may never fully understand, finds it right to send or allow trials, over a sleepy God who sometimes takes His eye off the ball.

Two "In Bounds" Options

1) God is sovereign over all things, and inscrutable, wise, holy, and good in all that He does. He wills our sanctification, and in so doing, values our holiness above our temporal happiness. Therefore, He who works all things for His glory and our good (e.g. Romans 8:28) sends both pleasant and painful things upon all people, as He deems fit— especially His redeemed children.

This position does not leave us free from any questions. Nor is it a fatalistic position which absolves us from the biblical duties to pray, alleviate suffering whenever possible, and war against our enemy, Satan. What it does do is place us in a position where we have to activate true faith and grapple with mysteries by thinking biblically while being convinced of the essential sovereign goodness and wisdom of our Heavenly Father.

I can live with this position while I await a clearer day. It invites me into a universe that ultimately makes sense, and into a life of faith where I finally trust and rest in the good providence of God, even while living in these "shadowlands."

2) We live in a fallen world, and as such, there are "natural" consequences to our fallenness from which God does not always deem it right to protect us. This view, being similar to the one above, recognizes that we live every moment in dependence upon God's providential mercy and sustaining grace. God carefully protects His Creation, and nothing gets to His children without first crossing His desk. As such, He protects us moment by moment from a myriad of dangers which exist as natural consequences of our fallen state. (What mercy!)

However, in His wisdom, He may deem it right to withdraw His protective hand and allow painful events to "naturally" run their course, coming upon us either as chastisement, for our sanctification, or to redirect our path (Galatians 4:13). He will sometimes allow the consequences of our bad choices to be visited upon us, even as He so often shields us from getting what we really deserve.

I can also live with this position, believing that it preserves the Bible's teaching that God is ultimately in control, even as He rules over a Creation which is temporarily subject to the "natural" consequences of the Fall (Romans 8:19-20).

I offer the above for your consideration. My primary concern is that we all strive to think biblically. While requiring diligence and hard work, this will preserve us from sub-Christian views of God and life, superstition, and heretical teaching. Biblical thinking will bring us all to a place where we can prosper in the midst of this life, even as we await a day when we shall know fully even as we are fully known (1 Corinthians 13:12).

I leave you with the poetic and pure theology of William Cowper, God's suffering hymnwriter:

****

God Of My Life, to Thee I Call

God of my life, to Thee I call;
Afflicted, at Thy feet I fall;
When the great water floods prevail
Leave not my trembling heart to fail!

Friend of the friendless and the saint,
Where should I lodge my deep complaint?
Where but with Thee, whose open door
Invites the helpless and the poor!

Did ever mourner plead with Thee,
And Thou refuse that mourner's plea?
Does not the Word still fixed remain
That none shall seek Thy face in vain?

That were a grief I could not bear,
Didst Thou not hear and answer prayer;
But a prayer hearing, answering God
Supports me under every load.

Fair is the lot that's cast for me!
I have an Advocate with Thee;
They whom the world caresses most,
Have no such privilege to boast.

Poor though I am, despised, forgot,
Yet God, my God, forgets me not;
And he is safe, and must succeed,
For whom the Lord vouchsafes to plead.

(William Cowper, 1731-1800)

Letter 28

Consider Him Who is More Than Enough

Yet I am always with you;
*   you hold me by my right hand.*
You guide me with your counsel,
*   and afterward you will take me into glory.*
Whom have I in heaven but you?
*   And earth has nothing I desire besides you.*
My flesh and my heart may fail,
*   but God is the strength of my heart*
*   and my portion forever.* (Psalm 73:23-26)

Dear Friend in Jesus,

I read today of a college football coach who just signed a multimillion dollar contract to coach young men at a prestigious university. Just two years ago, this very same man was fired from another university for having an affair with a young secretary and lying about it. Today, he is rewarded with an enviable coaching position. He will make much more money in a year than I will in a lifetime.

It bugs me.

Actually, it makes me mad.

Why is he prospering? He has a history of indiscretions, yet he is being given the responsibility and job of leading young men, while he has made it plain to all that he cannot even lead himself!

Life is not fair.

It can get to you if you let it.

It got to Asaph, a man in the Bible. He tells us all about it in Psalm 73:

> But as for me, my feet had almost slipped;
> I had nearly lost my foothold.
> For I envied the arrogant
> when I saw the prosperity of the wicked.
>
> They have no struggles;
> their bodies are healthy and strong.
> They are free from common human burdens;
> they are not plagued by human ills.
> Therefore pride is their necklace;
> they clothe themselves with violence.
> From their callous hearts comes iniquity;
> their evil imaginations have no limits.
> They scoff, and speak with malice;
> with arrogance they threaten oppression.
> Their mouths lay claim to heaven,
> and their tongues take possession of the earth.
> Therefore their people turn to them
> and drink up waters in abundance.
> They say, "How would God know?
> Does the Most High know anything?"
>
> This is what the wicked are like—
> always free of care, they go on amassing wealth.
> (Psalm 73:2-12)

I am not going to walk through these insightful verses with you. You can read them. The pictures they paint of the carefree partier are timeless. Take some time over them; it will be well worth the effort.

I am vexed...not only by the football coach above; I am also thinking of a football player who dodged a rape charge this past year.

Having won everything in sight, his stock is (still) sky high. People think he is a hero—I don't. I think he is a jerk. At the same time, one of my sons was in the hospital with multiple skull fractures for heroically saving a woman from a drunken thug on the street who then turned on my son. He is a true hero, but he suffers for his heroism.

Unfair.

To dwell upon such inequalities can really turn one's head around. With his head spinning, Asaph writes:

> Surely in vain I have kept my heart pure
> and have washed my hands in innocence.
> All day long I have been afflicted,
> and every morning brings new punishments.
>
> If I had spoken out like that,
> I would have betrayed your children.
> When I tried to understand all this,
> it troubled me deeply. (Psalm 73:13-16)

Read what he said! I *know* you have felt like he felt! I have. *What is the use of following Jesus? What good has it done me to pursue an upright life? Here is a guy who messes with women, puts himself first as a policy for life, lies when it suits his cause, and look at him... smiling on the front of some glossy magazine because he won a ball game...and I am not sure if I can afford to fix my car!*

It is all pretty bleak...until we begin to look at things and think in the light of eternity. Then *everything* changes. *EVERYTHING CHANGES*. These guys are not getting away with anything. Their pleasure is short-lived, and their day in court is looming:

> When I tried to understand all this,
> it troubled me deeply
> till I entered the sanctuary of God;
> then I understood their final destiny.

> Surely you place them on slippery ground;
> you cast them down to ruin.
> How suddenly are they destroyed,
> completely swept away by terrors!
> They are like a dream when one awakes;
> when you arise, Lord,
> you will despise them as fantasies.
>
> When my heart was grieved
> and my spirit embittered,
> I was senseless and ignorant;
> I was a brute beast before you.
> (Psalm 73:16-22)

Failure to get God's perspective on mundane matters can leave one embittered and beastlike. Spending some time with God (which invariably involves an open Bible)—what Asaph called "entering the sanctuary of God"—is revolutionary to the embattled believer. That football coach is "on slippery ground." Rather than envy him, admire him, or be incensed at him, I need to pity him...and pray for him! He needs Jesus. He is in BIG trouble. That gloating rapist-turned-trophy-winner on that magazine cover is about to be "swept away by terrors."

Okay, so they are getting their glory now. *This is as good as it gets for them.* Unless they turn to Jesus in true repentance, there can be no long-term hope for them. For the simple believer in Jesus, our glory is delayed, but sure to come. *This is as bad as it gets for us!* Our reward is nothing less than Jesus Christ Himself. Jesus Christ is *more than enough* for the Christian. He has to be. He must be.

> Yet I am always with you;
> you hold me by my right hand.
> You guide me with your counsel,
> and afterward you will take me into glory.

Whom have I in heaven but you?
And earth has nothing I desire besides you.
My flesh and my heart may fail,
but God is the strength of my heart
and my portion forever. (Psalm 73:23-26)

We get Jesus, and Jesus gets us—period. He is our treasured reward, and we are His. However, when we get Him, we get everything else, too. As C.S. Lewis said:

"Aim at Heaven, and you get earth thrown in. Aim at earth, and you get neither."

Just meditate...chew on Asaph's breakthrough in the verses above. This man lived in the dimmer light of the Old Testament. He did not know what you know. Yet he *got* what you might be *missing*:

God is...my portion forever. (Psalm 73:26)

The day will come...it *will* come...when we will bless every trial that weaned us from the fleeting shadows of this world's toys and moved us closer to Jesus Christ, our true and only treasure. For Jesus is not the means to an end. He *is* the goal and the prize. He *is* the treasure and the satisfaction. He *is* the whole gift...packaging, ribbon, and contents. So I have to say this: If you envy the godless secretly—even a little bit—you betray an ungrateful, unbelieving, divided, adulterous heart. You had best heed the warning of Jesus regarding an envious woman:

"Remember Lot's wife!" (Luke 17:32)

Those who are far from you will perish;
you destroy all who are unfaithful to you.
But as for me, it is good to be near God.

I have made the Sovereign Lord my refuge;
I will tell of all your deeds. (Psalm 73:27-28)

Asaph went into the sanctuary confused, envious, and embittered. He came out a different man. The one who almost lost his way comes forth having been "near God," and is ready to speak of the goodness of his God.

****

There Is Joy in My Soul

There is joy in my soul, for the Savior is mine,
I am wearing the pledge of His Spirit divine;
Every promise by faith through His grace I may claim,
Oh, His love passeth knowledge, all praise to His Name.

> *There is joy in my soul, there is joy in my song,*
> *I am nearing the gates of the bright, shining throng;*
> *And I list to the music of Eden so fair,*
> *Hallelujah to Jesus, I soon shall be there.*

There is joy in my soul that will never depart,
My Redeemer has made His abode in my heart;
From the tempter and sin I am kept every hour,
Oh, His love passeth knowledge, so great is its power.

There is joy in my soul though the clouds may arise,
Yet the bow of His mercy ne'er fades from the skies;
I am standing by faith where the pure waters glide,
Oh, His love passeth knowledge, so deep and so wide

There is joy in my soul, there is rapture and rest,
In my Savior and Lord I am perfectly blest;

'Twill be only a step 'ere my feet press the shore,
Then "His love passeth knowledge," I'll shout evermore.

There is joy in my soul, there is joy in my song,
I am nearing the gates of the bright, shining throng;
And I list to the music of Eden so fair,
Hallelujah to Jesus, I soon shall be there.

(Fanny Crosby, 1820-1915)

Letter 29

Consider Him Who Is in All Ways Wonderful

*For unto us a child is born, unto us a son is given: and the
government shall be upon his shoulder: and his name shall
be called Wonderful, Counsellor, The mighty God, The everlasting Father, The Prince of Peace. Of the increase of his
government and peace there shall be no end, upon the throne
of David, and upon his kingdom, to order it, and to establish
it with judgment and with justice from henceforth even for
ever. The zeal of the Lord of hosts will perform this.*
(Isaiah 9:6-7, KJV)

Dear Fellow Follower,

Indescribably wonderful. Beyond the power of any words to express.
Jesus Christ, the Bible's Christ, takes us to the very edge of all we can
comprehend and leaves us awestruck.

That is what is supposed to happen, for:

**What you think about when you think about Jesus Christ is the
most important thing about you.**

The health of your soul is determined by the value of that which
it loves the most.

The best thing you can do for yourself, your family, your culture,
your generation, is to expand your knowledge and experience of Jesus
Christ.

The greatest need of my life, and of yours, is to know the Bible's Jesus in greater depth and truth, for Jesus Christ is in all ways wonderful.

Isaiah's prophetic exaltation of Jesus (Isaiah 9:6-7, KJV), read in countless churches and homes every Christmas season, soars to the heights with its naming of our Saviour. We need to soar with it. We have spent enough time scratching among the turkeys in the barn-yard, when God would have us soar with the eagles! What follows can never do justice to the passage, but we might at least ascend through the murky fog of the turkey zone as we aspire to the eagle country heights above the clouds.

Jesus!

The eternal Son of God is *born,* is *given...unto us.* As my words fail, ask God the Holy Spirit to affect you with this. God...becomes a baby, a Son who is given for us. He shoulders the government of all history. This one rules over a kingdom that is yet and not yet, here and not here, seen and unseen, temporal and eternal. He will never resign, grow weary, use indiscretion, or offend truth and right. He is incor-ruptible and unimpeachable.

Jesus!

What's in a name? In the world of the Bible, everything is in a name. A name describes. A name defines. A name details. We understand a person when we understand his or her name. The Holy Spirit, through the prophet's pen, gives our Lord Jesus a five-faceted name. Each facet belongs solely to God, and each facet is given to Jesus Christ.

Wonderful

Wonderful literally means *miraculous, extraordinary, astonishing, separate, and distinguished.* These words describe and define Jesus Christ in terms of who He is, and in terms of His saving acts and work. He who will one day be marveled at high and low is to be marveled at by His Church here and now.

Many, Lord my God, are the wonders you have done, the things you planned for us.

None can compare with you; were I to speak and tell of your deeds, they would be too many to declare. (Psalm 40:5)

Counselor

Here is wisdom available to all who will ask. Here is the one who understands the heart. Here is the one who sees the problem and knows the remedy. The word means *advisor: one who admonishes; one who plans and purposes*. So Jesus not only has the wisdom to *will*, but the wherewithal to *do* what He purposes. *This* counselor does not merely nod His head and tut-tut at the troubled world; *this* counselor thwarts the wicked and secures His purposes. Be sure of it.

> The Lord bringeth the counsel of the heathen to nought:
>> he maketh the devices of the people of none effect.
> The counsel of the Lord standeth for ever,
>> the thoughts of his heart to all generations.
> (Psalm 33:10-11, KJV)

The Mighty God

Note that all-important word, *The*. There is no other Mighty God. The God of the Bible—Father, Son, and Holy Spirit—stands alone. This is a military title. Jesus is a warrior. Jesus is not a wimpy Western male. He is the *real* superhero. Jesus hates evil and He *will* triumph over it. Evil will *never* win. Count on it.

> Gird your sword on your side, you mighty one;
>> clothe yourself with splendor and majesty.
> In your majesty ride forth victoriously
>> in the cause of truth, humility and justice;
>> let your right hand achieve awesome deeds.
> Let your sharp arrows pierce the hearts of the king's enemies;
>> let the nations fall beneath your feet. (Psalm 45:3-5)

The Everlasting Father

Don't get confused here, but do be amazed! Don't let this amazing name take you to a heresy called "modalism" ("**Modalism,** also called **Sabellianism,** is the unorthodox belief that God is one person who has revealed himself in three forms or *modes* in contrast to the Trinitarian doctrine where God is one being eternally existing in three persons." [37]). Jonathan Edwards, speaking of this verse, writes:

> "It shows a wonderful conjunction of excellencies, that the same person should be a Son, born and given, and yet be the everlasting Father, without beginning or end; that he should be a Child, and yet be he whose name is Counsellor, and the mighty God; and well may his name, in whom such things are conjoined, be called Wonderful."[38]

Jesus, coeternal and one with God the Father, the author of our eternal life, exercises fatherly care over us, and is the source and fount of all our blessings. He is enduring, patient, protective, and powerful. It is from Him that we derive all of our life and being.

> And again he says,
> "Here am I, and the children God has given me." (Hebrews 2:13)

> My sheep listen to my voice; I know them, and they follow me. I give them eternal life, and they shall never perish; no one will snatch them out of my hand. My Father, who has given them to me, is greater than all; no one can snatch them out of my Father's hand. I and the Father are one. (John 10:27-30)

The Prince of Peace

Here is the one who reconciles us to His Father. Here is the one who does what is otherwise impossible. Friend, if you and I had any meaningful understanding of what our *natural* enmity toward God was, and the peace Jesus has secured for us, we would be jumping for joy, weeping with gratitude, shouting with praise, dumb-struck with awe, and telling the world.

> Like the rest, we were by nature deserving of wrath. But because of his great love for us, God, who is rich in mercy, made us alive with Christ even when we were dead in transgressions—it is by grace you have been saved. (Ephesians 2:3-5)

Now, my words are weak. I pray that the Holy Spirit of God will open your heart and mind to the wonders of Jesus Christ. There is so much GLORY here! It is proclaimed, and what God purposes and proclaims, He accomplishes: "of the increase of the government of Jesus there shall be no end" (*c.f.* Isaiah 9:7). This is a Gospel declaration. The spread of the good news of Jesus will cover the earth! Indeed, it *is* covering the earth! The zeal of the Lord—bursting in the hearts of ordinary, mission-mad believers—will accomplish this increase, to the end that:

> The earth will be filled with the knowledge of the glory of the Lord as the waters cover the sea. (Habakkuk 2:14)

Oh, fellow follower of the Wonderful One, pray and seek for an alive, thriving heart. Considering Jesus is intended to stir the heart, change the mind, and motivate the life! I think the best I can do here is leave us with the prayer Matthew Henry (1662-1714) prayed at the end of his commentary on this passage:

> Give then, O Lord, to thy people, to know thee by every endearing name, and in every glorious character. Be thou to us, to all, our Wonderful Counsellor, our Mighty God, our Everlasting Father, our Prince of Peace! And since in ourselves and all our circumstances, we are nothing, can do nothing, and by reason

of sin are worse than nothing, be pleased to carry on thy work with power in our souls; and of the increase of thy government and peace, let there be no end. Let it be ever growing and still to grow. Give increase of grace, in every heart of thy redeemed upon the earth![39]

I just have to get the following hymn in. Once again, John Newton comes through! He who is forgiven much loves much, and he *understands* much. This hymn soars on the heights of Gospel truth as it extols the neverending reign of Jesus Christ. There have been times when I sang this hymn with a company of God's people, and the veil between things seen and unseen, temporary and eternal, shadowy and bright, grew wafer thin! Indeed, it was almost a disappointment to open my eyes at the end to find myself still in the "land of the living"!

****

Glorious Things of Thee Are Spoken

> Glorious things of thee are spoken,
> Zion, city of our God;
> he whose word cannot be broken
> formed thee for his own abode;
> on the Rock of Ages founded,
> what can shake thy sure repose?
> With salvation's walls surrounded,
> thou may'st smile at all thy foes.
>
> See! the streams of living waters,
> springing from eternal love,
> well supply thy sons and daughters
> and all fear of want remove.
> Who can faint, when such a river
> ever flows their thirst to assuage?
> Grace which, like the Lord, the Giver,

never fails from age to age.

Round each habitation hovering,
see the cloud and fire appear
for a glory and a covering,
showing that the Lord is near.
Thus they march, their pillar leading,
light by night, and shade by day;
daily on the manna feeding
which he gives them when they pray.

Blest inhabitants of Zion,
washed in the Redeemer's blood!
Jesus, whom their souls rely on,
makes them kings and priests to God.
'Tis his love his people raises
over self to reign as kings:
and as priests, his solemn praises
each for a thank-offering brings.

Savior, if of Zion's city,
I through grace a member am,
let the world deride or pity,
I will glory in thy Name.
Fading is the worldling's pleasure,
all his boasted pomp and show;
solid joys and lasting treasure
none but Zion's children know.

(John Newton, 1725-1807)

Letter 30

Consider Him, the Desire of all Nations, Who Desires the Nations

And I will shake all nations, and the desire of all nations
shall come: and I will fill this house with glory, saith the Lord
of hosts. (Haggai 2:7, KJV)

Dear Friends,

We don't know what is good for us. We don't know what we really need. This is true not just on an individual level, but on a worldwide level. The nations are sick...and don't know it.

However, Jesus Christ has a plan!

Sick patients cannot self-diagnose, and they must not self-prescribe. Planet Earth is ill, and is incapable of a clear and accurate self-diagnosis. It follows that all its self-remedies will fail to bring the needed cure.

I think it is safe to say that all reasonable people and reasonable nations desire peace, prosperity, and safety. The vision of the old prophet Micah, God's vision for the nations, speaks to the heart of all peoples everywhere:

Everyone will sit under their own vine
and under their own fig tree,
and no one will make them afraid,
for the Lord Almighty has spoken.
(Micah 4:4)

On our own we just cannot do it. Having moved further and further away from God, we are adrift on the stormy seas of rebellion and headed towards wreck and ruin. Our world cannot live without God. Friedrich Nietzsche (1844-1900) reasoned that we had, in a moral and intellectual sense, killed God. Because ideas matter, this led him to the only logical end: insanity. He spent the last eleven years of his life "out of it." Why not? Indeed, as C.S. Lewis noted, when the Devil finishes with his tools, he breaks them. Through the frayed thoughts of an unraveling mind, Nietzsche prophesied that, mankind being engulfed in a universal madness where right would be wrong and wrong would be right, the godless twentieth century would become the bloodiest, most destructive century in history,. The ugly would replace the beautiful, and the unholy the holy.

So, here we are, in the wake of the bloodiest, maddest century ever, a century that lived and died on the bitter fruit of its poisoned thinking. It is impossible to get an exact count of the wars fought since the madman Nietzsche died in 1900, but it is estimated that at any given time, there are roughly *forty* wars being fought on this planet. Add to this the civil unrest, social upheaval, domestic dismemberment, economic earthquakes, and ecological catastrophes, and it is clear we are living on a broken planet.

Our politicians and sociologists, try as they may, cannot help because they have the wrong idea about things. They have failed to see the true problem: our corporate and individual rebellion against God. Our disease is deep. We have corrupt, evil hearts, and Jesus Christ is the only answer for every person, and every tribe, tongue, and nation. What the nations desire—peace, safety, cohesiveness—is available, but only in Jesus Christ. We are too sick to know what we need, and we are too foolish to see the remedy before us.

Jesus Christ is what we need.

   Jesus Christ is what we want.

      We are just too sick and wicked to know it.

Here is the twist in the tale: Not only is Jesus the "desire of the nations," but **the nations are the desire of Jesus Christ!** The heart of Jesus is for every tribe and tongue and nation to be redeemed from sin and whole, prosperous, and plentiful:

> And they sang a new song, saying: "You are worthy to take the scroll and to open its seals, because you were slain, and with your blood you purchased for God persons from every tribe and language and people and nation." (Revelation 5:9)

The early Gospel promise to Abraham, fulfilled in Jesus, was and is for every nation:

> "I will make you into a great nation, and I will bless you;
> I will make your name great, and you will be a blessing.
> I will bless those who bless you, and whoever curses you I will curse;
> and all peoples on earth will be blessed through you." (Genesis 12:2-3)

Thus the command of Jesus to His Church is that we go to every corner of the globe with His Gospel:

> Therefore go and make disciples of all nations, baptizing them in the name of the Father and of the Son and of the Holy Spirit, and teaching them to obey everything I have commanded you. And surely I am with you always, to the very end of the age. (Matthew 28:19-20)

At the close of history, Jesus will receive redeemed cultures and nations as His prize and reward:

> Ask me, and I will make the nations your inheritance, the ends of the earth your possession. (Psalm 2:8)

On no day will its gates ever be shut, for there will be no night there. The glory and honor of the nations will be brought into it. (Revelation 21:25-26)

The nations—too sick to know what is good for them—will only have their desires met in Jesus. And He desires the nations. He *loves* cultures. He loves skin colours, people groups, music styles, art forms, tastes, smells, and dances! In the Kingdom of God, cultures will not be abolished, but redeemed. Glory! Imagine the *best* of every nation, *minus* the sin factor.

Thus, once again, the truth that is in Jesus is radically different from *every other religious leader.* Take Islam. In this tragic religion, there is not an appreciable distinction between the religion and the culture. In varying degrees, in order to become Muslim, you have to abandon your culture and embrace the medieval culture of Islam. Jesus asked that you embrace *Him,* and then He will redeem both you and your culture, and make both beautiful.

Way to go Jesus!

Even today, every place where the Gospel is lived out in simplicity and truth, we see the beginnings of the redemption of cultures and peoples. It is imperfect at present and has often been terribly marred by us, but it is happening in seed now and will happen in full flower one day. I'm stepping into the Gospel parade with Jesus Christ. There is *no way* He is going to give up on this world. The blood He shed on the cross purchased all creation back, and He is going to have it... redeemed, glorious, perfect, and radiant.

This is the desire of Jesus, and He gets what He wants.

* * * * * * * * * *

O Come, O Come, Emmanuel

O come, O come, Emmanuel,
And ransom captive Israel,
That mourns in lonely exile here
Until the Son of God appear.

Rejoice! Rejoice!
Emmanuel shall come to thee, O Israel.

O come, Thou Wisdom from on high,
Who orderest all things mightily;
To us the path of knowledge show,
And teach us in her ways to go.

O come, Thou Rod of Jesse, free
Thine own from Satan's tyranny;
From depths of hell Thy people save,
And give them victory over the grave.

O come, Thou Day-spring, come and cheer
Our spirits by Thine advent here;
Disperse the gloomy clouds of night,
And death's dark shadows put to flight.

O come, Thou Key of David, come,
And open wide our heavenly home;
Make safe the way that leads on high,
And close the path to misery.

O come, O come, great Lord of might,
Who to Thy tribes on Sinai's height
In ancient times once gave the law
In cloud and majesty and awe.

O come, Thou Root of Jesse's tree,
An ensign of Thy people be;
Before Thee rulers silent fall;
All peoples on Thy mercy call.

O come, Desire of nations, bind
In one the hearts of all mankind;
Bid Thou our sad divisions cease,
And be Thyself our King of Peace.

Rejoice! Rejoice!
Emmanuel shall come to thee, O Israel.

(Twelfth Century, Author Unknown)

Letter 31

Consider Him Who Is the Cause of Endless Conflicts!

For I came to cast fire on earth. (Luke 12:49)

Beloved in Christ,

If what you think about when you think about Jesus Christ is the most important thing about you, then what the Church thinks about when it thinks about Jesus Christ is the most important thing about it. Individuals, churches, and entire cultures cannot and will never rise above their theology. We become like what we worship and value most. Entertain low views of God, and you will live accordingly. Pursue and be apprehended by the glorious God of the Bible, who has revealed Himself finally in Jesus Christ, and you will not only live accordingly, but be transformed on the inside. It is an inescapable law that we become like that which we worship. Ideas matter.

There has always been an effort to sentimentalize Jesus: to emasculate, reduce, and trivialize Him. There is always this pressure to make Him palatable. He is C.S. Lewis' Aslan; not "safe," but "good." He is not nice in the "cup of tea" sense of the word. He is presented in the Bible as Lord of Lords and King of Kings. Forasmuch as He is the Prince of Peace (and untold millions can so testify to His being just that to them), He is also the Great Disturber. He has been disturbing me for half a century. He literally ruined my life, but then again, my life needed ruining, for it was a Hell-bound life. He is the disturber of individuals, families, cultures, and nations. He is relentless in His mission to bring in His kingdom, and subdue all who challenge it.

Don't take my word on this, take it from Him:

"I have come to bring fire on the earth, and how I wish it were already kindled! But I have a baptism to undergo, and what constraint I am under until it is completed! Do you think I came to bring peace on earth? No, I tell you, but division. From now on there will be five in one family divided against each other, three against two and two against three. They will be divided, father against son and son against father, mother against daughter and daughter against mother, mother-in-law against daughter-in-law and daughter-in-law against mother-in-law." (Luke 12:49-53)

Without apology and without flinching, Jesus declares Himself to be *the* issue. The Prince of Peace picks a fight with all pretenders. Now we in the West in the early twenty-first century have real problems with the real Jesus. We are terribly squeamish in the presence of such boldness. We really do want a "nice" savior; one who embraces everyone, and just helps us live happier lives. And certainly in the "majority world," on the glorious frontiers of missions, the real Jesus is causing no end of problems. In lands where countless gods vie for space, or where followers of a tyrannical prophet live and die by the sword, or where atheistic ideology seeks to keep millions of minds in the vice of unbelief, the Bible's Jesus is a real troublemaker.

Why? Is Jesus just another militant agitator, or is something greater going on? Does the Prince of Peace who blesses "peacemakers" know something that we do not know (Isaiah 9:6, Matthew 5:9)?

In seeking answers, we must first agree that the Bible is a book about Jesus Christ. It tells us so:

And beginning with Moses and all the Prophets, he explained to them what was said in all the Scriptures concerning himself. (Luke 24:27)

You study the Scriptures diligently because you think that in them you have eternal life. These are the very Scriptures that testify about me. (John 5:39)

Then Philip began with that very passage of Scripture and told him the good news about Jesus. (Acts 8:35)

The Bible is not first and foremost a book about us. It is not primarily written to make us feel better, happier, or more successful. It is written to reveal God's Son to us, that we might believe in Him and be saved from sin and God's righteous wrath.

But these are written that you may believe that Jesus is the Messiah, the Son of God, and that by believing you may have life in his name. (John 20:31)

Whoever believes in the Son has eternal life, but whoever rejects the Son will not see life, for God's wrath remains on them. (John 3:36)

The Bible is relentless in making Jesus of Nazareth the pivotal issue of humanity, from individual to international level, and at every level in between. Without apology and with great certainty, it diagnoses the human condition and prescribes Christ as the remedy. He is both the goal and the prize of all genuine Christian endeavour, and in the New Testament He is unashamedly presented to the syncretistic, nationalistic, militaristic, pessimistic world the apostles (and company) encountered as the only way and the only hope.

"Salvation is found in no one else, for there is no other name under heaven given to mankind by which we must be saved."... Peter and John replied, "Which is right in God's eyes: to listen to you, or to him? You be the judges! As for us, we cannot help speaking about what we have seen and heard." (Acts 4:12, 19-20)

Jesus Himself, though "gentle and humble in heart" (Matthew 11:29), recognized and acknowledged the importance of His person-hood and His mission:

"I am the way and the truth and the life. No one comes to the Father except through me." (John 14:6)

"For the Son of Man came to seek and to save the lost." (Luke 19:10)

Statements such as these are profound, both in regards to what Jesus Christ is saying about Himself, and about us. He is certain that we are in great trouble, and cannot help ourselves, for we are lost and need to be saved. He has come to do it, and *no one else can.*

Open upon my desk is my dog-eared copy of Josh McDowell's, *Evidence That Demands a Verdict.* I bought the book in 1975 as a university freshman, as I was grappling with Jesus, who was beginning to rearrange my life. It was in his chapter "The Trilema—Lord, Liar, or Lunatic" that I first read and was arrested by the famous words of C.S. Lewis:

I am trying here to prevent anyone saying the really foolish thing that people often say about Him: "I am ready to accept Jesus as a great moral teacher, but I don't accept His claim to be God." That is the one thing we must not say. A man who was merely a man and said the sort of things Jesus said would not be a great moral teacher. He would either be a lunatic—on the level with a man who says he is a poached egg—or else he would be the Devil of Hell. You must make your choice. Either the man was, and is, the Son of God: or else a madman or something worse...You can shut Him up for a fool, you can spit at Him and kill Him as a demon; or you can fall at His feet and call Him Lord and God. But let's not come up with any of that patronizing nonsense about His being a great human teacher. He has not left that open to us. He did not intend to.[40]

The Jesus of the Bible simply does not leave space for ambivalence. We just cannot shrug our shoulders and walk away. Today's world loves, even applauds, vagueness where truth is concerned, because we are all desperately afraid of offending anyone. Jesus—the real Jesus—does not fit. He cannot. The diagnosis itself is "offensive." "Lost? Not me!" "Chief not lost—teepee lost!" The confidence Jesus has in Himself to do something about our calamity is tolerable until the definite article "the" pops up, and we realize that Jesus claims to *be the only one* who can help us out of our mess. The whole direction of the Bible is calculated to force a decision about Jesus. It prods us. It hounds the human race in its invitation/ultimatum to believe and be saved. It is relentless in its witness to Christ.

So must the faithful Church be in this challenging century.

We want a god we can control, reduce, get our minds around, and enlist on our side. Jesus just won't play. The Jesus of the Bible is beyond anything we could ever have dreamed. He is for people we thought he would never be for, and He stands against people we would have thought He would never stand against. In some ways, He just does not act the way we imagine a god should act. He eats with "bad" people and makes all the "good" people mad at Him. He sometimes seems to do things on purpose just to get the "good" people mad!

He certainly is not religious.

The big issue regarding Jesus Christ pivots on the question, "Who is He?" The Bible presents enough data to arrive at a clear, concise, and astounding conclusion: Jesus Christ is the unique and only Son of God, the Judge of all, and the Saviour of sinners.

Now, because this conclusion is unpalatable to so many—it being neither politically correct nor inclusive—numerous answers to the question, "Who is He?" have been proposed. None of them is potent enough to upset anyone. Each sub-Christian view presents a paler, more user-friendly Jesus; attractive to various interest groups in one way or another, but worthy of neither worship nor radical, costly following. Each may have aspects of truth, but none present a complete picture of who Jesus is.

Jesus the Mistaken Martyr

Here is a Jesus swept up in the events that surround him. Jerusalem is a cauldron of revolution and rebellion. Jesus is a well-meaning pacifist, caught up in the moment. He is not in control of events; events are in control of Him. Jesus is stitched up by zealous and jealous Jews, and falsely accused of leading a rebellion. Being a man of peace, He would rather suffer for peace and die than fight back. The premise of this position is that we need to aspire to higher ideals, as exemplified by Jesus. He dies mistaken, but valiant...an inspiration for all.

Jesus the Guru/Teacher

With very little imagination we can see this Jesus reverently sitting alongside the Maharishi Mahesh Yogi, with John, Paul, George, and Ringo at his feet as He offers wisdom and advice for life. We actually hear people say: "I love the teachings of Jesus. I try to live my life by them every day" (which is a sure clue that they have never read them). Some may even tag Jesus as "the greatest teacher ever." The premise of this view is that people basically need teaching/correcting, but not saving. We are not fundamentally sinful, just ignorant.

Jesus the Liberator

We see here a Jesus (perhaps wearing worn military fatigues) who is a champion of the structurally oppressed. He wages an ideological war against social structures by which the rich oppress the poor. He serves our goal of releasing us from the shackles (usually capitalist) that keep us from realizing our potential. The revolutionary Jesus tells us that the problem with mankind is social sin, not a sinful nature in man. The premise here is that the problem is outside of man, with societies' structures, not with the heart of man.

Jesus the Prophet

Here is a Jesus who undoubtedly speaks from God. We can line him up with Moses or Muhammad. This Jesus is no ordinary man. He is a spokesman, perhaps even the greatest spokesman (unless one is a Muslim, accepting Jesus as a prophet, though subordinate to Muhammad). What an accolade! Jesus the prophet! The premise here is that the human race can, is willing—even needs—to hear from God. If God will just speak to us through His prophets, we will hear and do what He says.

The list above could go on and on: Jesus the Capitalist, Jesus the Republican, Jesus the White Man, Jesus the One Who Promises Me Success, Jesus the Socialist, Jesus the _____, and so on. The bottom line is: We must be very careful that we do not invent a Jesus of our own fancy, one who serves our purposes—a mascot rather than a master. That would be idolatry, even if it exists only in our thoughts ("I like to think of Jesus *this* way..."). Ideas matter.

The neverending challenge is to *let the Bible tell us who Jesus is*, and then *deal* with *that* Jesus. Certainly Jesus' demeanour at death is an inspiration to us. Yes, His teachings and wisdom can help us in life. Certainly He sets people free, His Gospel can transform social structures, and yes, He speaks words which seem to pierce our hearts. However, all the "designer Jesuses" are here to somehow do what *we* want Him to do. There is nothing eternal, transcendent, breathtaking, offensive, unexplainable, dividing, or redeeming about any of them.

The current landscape is a challenging one, so far as truth is concerned. The flavour in fashion is best defined as pluralism, and truth struggles to be heard in an age committed to pluralism. Pluralism pretends that all views are equally valid, even if mutually exclusive. It thrives in a subjective, postmodern age in which the individual is his own source of authority in matters of right and wrong, and truth and falsehood, and trusts that there is nothing objectively "out there" that is absolutely true outside of himself.

Now, we all want to live in reasonable peace and harmony. We all want to be loving and kind towards those who believe differently from us. However, the cost of losing truth to pluralism is far too high. In the New Testament, the apostles were not afraid to say that certain things were *not* valid beliefs. According to them, there is truth and there is untruth. In the New Testament world, it is unloving to pretend something is true when it is not. It is loving to tell people about Jesus, even if it upsets them or gets us in trouble.

Donald Bloesch writes:

> The mood today is pluralistic and inclusivistic, and any claims to absolute truth are peremptorily dismissed by the academic elite. Those who would reaffirm orthodox Christology must take into serious consideration the radical relativism and historicism that pervade the intellectual life of the West.[41]

Of course such unbounded thinking is not found only in the West. A clear example of hazy Christological pluralism is presented by Indian theologian S.J. Samartha. The title of his book, *One Christ, Many Religions: Towards a Revised Christology,* tells you where he is going. He asserts:

> ...in a religiously plural world to be Christ-centred is not the only way to be God-centred.[42]

Oops. He just stepped out of bounds. He is no longer on the field of play.

Pluralism quickly pushes the "arrogant" button when a Christian who is confident in Christ comes along. The postmodern mind cannot stomach anything of absolute truth external from itself, so it has no category for the confident Christian, other than "narrow-minded" or "arrogant." It is an interesting turn of the tables, for in fact, it is in the very nature of postmodernism to place the umpire for truth and falsehood in the individual. The individual becomes the authoritative determiner of what is "true for him," which is really the very height of arrogance.

We need to recall the difference between *arrogance* and *confidence.* It needs to be said (probably again and again), that the faithful Christian is really not saying *anything* about himself. He is saying something about Jesus Christ. He is not saying, "I am right!" but saying, "Christ is right." The Christian is a member of the human race, and as such, he too is wrong and needs help. He is claiming something confidently about Jesus, but nothing confidently about himself... except that he needs help!

So, the big point of pluralism is that there is no such thing as absolute truth (though if there happens to be, it is unknowable anyway). So when Christianity comes along and presents itself not so much as a religion or philosophy, but as a history, it presents propositional truth and invites investigation. (See Luke 1:1-4; 3:1-2; 2 Peter 1:16-18; 1 John 1:1-4.) It is at the opposite end of the spectrum as far as the theory of knowledge goes, for it presents four things which are incompatible with (and therefore in conflict with) the pluralism of our age:

1. Truth exists.

2. Truth is knowable.

3. Jesus Christ is that truth incarnate.

4. The Bible is a faithful record of the truth that is Jesus Christ.

These four propositions are in profound conflict with the academic, philosophical spirit of our age; a spirit which has trickled right down to the man on the street. Along comes Jesus, and it is inevitable that sparks will fly, but fly they must. Although we who follow Jesus are called to lives of gentleness, we are not called to lives of spinelessness. We need to allow Jesus to be Jesus and not shy away from the fray *He* causes.

Yes, you read me right: Jesus *Himself* causes these conflicts. Put it all down to the things He said about *Himself*. People can try to invent a Jesus who takes His place alongside other meaningful figures of history, but the Jesus of the Bible just won't stay where people want Him to stay.

The bottom line is that this Jesus of history, this Jesus of the Bible, is the one who speaks to the need of mankind, and in so doing, answers the very cries of the human heart. The cries for meaning, purpose, redemption, forgiveness, belonging, reconciliation, justice, mercy, peace, deliverance, wholeness, renewal, and direction: all are met in Jesus Christ. Our motive for being faithful to Christian truth in our age is not that we want to be right, but that we want Jesus to be rightly honoured, discovered, and experienced in individual lives and entire cultures as *the* hope of mankind. *People need the Lord.* It should be our love for Christ and our corresponding love for others that compel us to be faithful to this generation by being faithful to Christ, no matter what the cost may be to us.

The conflicts Christ provokes are inevitable. They are akin to the conflicts a loving surgeon provokes...one whose sole goal is to heal patients. They are perhaps akin to those which a righteous general provokes...one whose sole aim is to liberate a people. These conflicts are temporary necessities. They are conflicts not of swords and bullets, but much deeper and more significant, of ideas and concepts, and finally of truth versus falsehood.

Don't dilute Jesus. The world needs to take Him "straight." Don't feel a need to defend Jesus. He can handle Himself just fine. Follow Him, proclaim Him, don't flinch when the sparks fly, and just see what He can do. One day, all will see Him and confess that He is Lord of all. Our privilege and challenge is to do so now.

****

Crown Him with Many Crowns

Crown Him with many crowns, the Lamb upon His throne.
Hark! How the heavenly anthem drowns all music but its own.
Awake, my soul, and sing of Him who died for thee,
And hail Him as thy matchless King through all eternity.

Crown Him the virgin's Son, the God incarnate born,
Whose arm those crimson trophies won which now His brow adorn;

Fruit of the mystic rose, as of that rose the stem;
The root whence mercy ever flows, the Babe of Bethlehem.

Crown Him the Son of God, before the worlds began,
And ye who tread where He hath trod, crown Him the Son of Man;
Who every grief hath known that wrings the human breast,
And takes and bears them for His own, that all in Him may rest.

Crown Him the Lord of life, who triumphed over the grave,
And rose victorious in the strife for those He came to save.
His glories now we sing, who died, and rose on high,
Who died eternal life to bring, and lives that death may die.

Crown Him the Lord of peace, whose power a scepter sways
From pole to pole, that wars may cease, and all be prayer and praise.
His reign shall know no end, and round His pierced feet
Fair flowers of paradise extend their fragrance ever sweet.

Crown Him the Lord of love, behold His hands and side,
Those wounds, yet visible above, in beauty glorified.
No angel in the sky can fully bear that sight,
But downward bends his burning eye at mysteries so bright.

Crown Him the Lord of Heaven, enthroned in worlds above,
Crown Him the King to Whom is given the wondrous name of Love.
Crown Him with many crowns, as thrones before Him fall;
Crown Him, ye kings, with many crowns, for He is King of all.

Crown Him the Lord of lords, who over all doth reign,
Who once on earth, the incarnate Word, for ransomed sinners slain,
Now lives in realms of light, where saints with angels sing
Their songs before Him day and night, their God, Redeemer, King.

Crown Him the Lord of years, the Potentate of time,
Creator of the rolling spheres, ineffably sublime.
All hail, Redeemer, hail! For Thou has died for me;
Thy praise and glory shall not fail throughout eternity.

(Matthew Bridges, 1800-1894)

Postscript

It has been a joy and privilege to sit and write these letters to you. Truly, they have come straight from my heart, and I hope they went straight into yours. I do not think it is possible to overstate the need of the hour. Our culture is in desperate need of a turn towards Christ. The nations are hurtling at breakneck speed towards conflict and calamity. Our universities and academic institutions are confused at their very foundations, being unsure about truth itself. We have spent and played and entertained our nations into bankruptcy. Marriage, the home, and family are being attacked through the subtle but sinister ploy of redefinition. Radical Islam is watching, waiting, plotting, and planning its move to dominate the entire globe. Our leaders, far from having any remedy, cannot even diagnose the problem.

We are living in perfect days for Jesus and His Gospel! He does well in stormy seas! It is *not* time to despair, but to live valiantly for Jesus. But ideas precede actions. Right living cannot come from wrong thinking. When we think right, we will find ourselves empowered to battle in the market-place of ideas. In the century ahead, some of us will suffer, some will be marginalized by a culture whose mind is closing shut, some will be martyred. What we won't be anymore is complacent.

These days will *prove* the true affections of our hearts, as we see the idols of personal peace and prosperity tumble. Jesus' counsel for those alive in the calamitous end times is clear:

> When these things begin to take place, stand up and lift up your heads, because your redemption is drawing near. (Luke 21:28)

Now is *not* the time to hang our heads! These are *not* days for backpedalling. God is not losing sleep, biting His nails, pacing the floor, or wringing His hands. In a very real sense, the very last thing we have to worry about is Christ and His kingdom. They are sure to come! However, we are called to usher in Christ's kingdom and to labour, at whatever the cost, for the spread of the Gospel. Francis Schaeffer warned (prophetically?) that the greatest threat to the Gospel in our day would be the dulling lure of what he called, "personal peace and prosperity." In other words, as long as I can close the door on a needy world, flop on the sofa, turn on the tube, and have my private faith, the world can go to Hell. This deadly attitude will cost us not only our culture and the advance of the Gospel in our day, but is out-and-out disobedience to Christ and His upward call.

I want no part of it for me. I want no part of it for you. I am convinced that the key to valiant living in these days boils down to being captivated by Jesus, His Gospel, and His kingdom. By God's grace, I am on a neverending journey of discovery with Christ. However, I am just one of hundreds of thousands—*millions*—from every tribe, tongue, and nation, who, by grace, has chosen to treasure Christ and His kingdom above all else.

Come with us! There is plenty of room for you—weaknesses, brokenness, quirks and all—in this great work and in these great days!

Yours for Christ and His Gospel,

John Gillespie

****

For All the Saints

For all the saints, who from their labors rest,
Who Thee by faith before the world confessed,
Thy Name, O Jesus, be forever blessed.
Alleluia, Alleluia!

Thou wast their Rock, their Fortress and their Might;
Thou, Lord, their Captain in the well fought fight;
Thou, in the darkness drear, their one true Light.
Alleluia, Alleluia!

For the Apostles' glorious company,
Who bearing forth the Cross o'er land and sea,
Shook all the mighty world, we sing to Thee:
Alleluia, Alleluia!

For Martyrs, who with rapture kindled eye,
Saw the bright crown descending from the sky,
And seeing, grasped it, Thee we glorify.
Alleluia, Alleluia!

O blest communion, fellowship divine!
We feebly struggle, they in glory shine;
All are one in Thee, for all are Thine.
Alleluia, Alleluia!

O may Thy soldiers, faithful, true and bold,
Fight as the saints who nobly fought of old,
And win with them the victor's crown of gold.
Alleluia, Alleluia!

And when the strife is fierce, the warfare long,
Steals on the ear the distant triumph song,

And hearts are brave, again, and arms are strong.
Alleluia, Alleluia!

The golden evening brightens in the west;
Soon, soon to faithful warriors comes their rest;
Sweet is the calm of paradise the blessed.
Alleluia, Alleluia!

But lo! there breaks a yet more glorious day;
The saints triumphant rise in bright array;
The King of glory passes on His way.
Alleluia, Alleluia!

From earth's wide bounds, from ocean's farthest coast,
Through gates of pearl streams in the countless host,
And singing to Father, Son and Holy Ghost:
Alleluia, Alleluia!

(William W. How, 1823-1897)

Notes

[1] Arnold Toynbee, http://www.brainyquote.com/quotes/authors/a/arnold_j_toynbee.html

[2] See Frederick Grossmith, *The Cross and the Swastika*, (Stamford: Paul Watkins Publishing, 1998). Also, Don Stephens, *War and Grace* (Darlington, Evangelical Press, 2005) 253-272.

[3] Ibid. Stephens, p. 262.

[4] At one level or another, I too am guilty of all these crimes…so are you.

[5] *Ibid*. p. 269.

[6] *Ibid*. p. 269.

[7] Martin Luther, *A Commentary on St. Paul's Epistle to the Galatians,* (Cambridge: James Clarke & Co., 1953) 164.

[8] Jonathan Edwards, http://www.ccel.org/ccel/edwards/sermons.excellency.html

[9] *Ibid.*

[10] John Piper, http://www.desiringgod.org/biographies/you-will-be-eaten-by-cannibals-lessons-from-the-life-of-john-g-paton

[11] John Foxe, *Foxe's Book of Martyrs,* (Grand Rapids: Zondervan, 1926) 9.

[12] Aldous Huxley, "Confessions of a Professed Atheist," Report: Perspective on the News, Volume 3, June 1966, page 19 (italics added).

[13] C.S. Lewis, *Surprised by Joy*, (Glasgow: Collins Sons and Co. Ltd., 1955) 182.

[14] *Ibid.*

[15] I found these words scribbled in some of my old sermon notes. I don't know where I got them! They sound like something Roy Hession would say. Then again, maybe I had a particularly good moment!

[16] Augustine of Hippo, *Confessions* (Nashville: Thomas Nelson Publishers, 1999) 230.

[17] http://www.patheos.com/Library/Glossary/Pelagianism.html

[18] Dietrich Bonhoeffer, *Life Together* (San Francisco: Harper & Row, 1954) 67,68 (brackets added).

[19] An Epicurean is one given over to the pursuit of pleasure, especially in the realm of foods.

[20] Jonathan Edwards, "Sinners in the Hands of an Angry God,*" The Works of Jonathan Edwards*) *Volume 2* (Edinburgh: The Banner of Truth Trust, 1974) 9.

[21] http://www.theopedia.com/Christus_Victor

[22] Calvin Miller, *Into the Depths of God* (Minneapolis: Bethany House Publishers, 2000) 156.

[23] J.C. Ryle, *Luke* (Nottingham: Crossway Books, 1997) 301.

[24] Jonathan Edwards, "The Excellency of Christ," *The Works of Jonathan Edwards, Volume 1* (Edinburgh: The Banner of Truth Trust, 1974) 685.

[25] Miller, *op.cit.,* 164.

[26] C.S. Lewis, *Mere Christianity* (San Francisco: Harper Collins 2001) 216.

[27] *Ibid*. p. 206.

[28] *Ibid*. p. 196.

[29] http://www.cyberhymnal.org/bio/c/r/o/crosby_fj.htm

[30] John Calvin, *Institutes of the Christian Religion,* (Westminster: John Knox Press, 1960) 2.16.19.

[31] Luther, *op. cit.*, p.170.

[32] Foxe, *op. cit.,* p. 237.

[33] Read about her at http://www.stempublishing.com/hymns/biographies/cherry.html.

[34] Dietrich Bonhoeffer, *The Cost of Discipleship* (New York: MacMillan Publishing, 1959) 45-47 (bracket added).

[35] James Townsend, http://www.christianitytoday.com/ch/1991/issue31/3100.html

[36] This letter was written to my then congregation, Grace Community Church, Cornwall, in the aftermath of the 2011 Japan Tsunami.

[37] http://www.theopedia.com/Modalism. Author's name not supplied.

[38] Jonathan Edwards, "The Excellency of Christ," *The Works of Jonathan Edwards, Volume 1* (Edinburgh: The Banner of Truth Trust, 1974) 686.

[39] Henry's writings were of huge worth to George Whitefield's spiritual formation. He writes: "For many months I have been almost always upon my knees, to study and pray over [Matthew Henry's Commentary]." I think it can be said that, at least in a significant part, the great Eighteenth Century Awakening was birthed in the heart of a young man (Whitefield) on his knees before Henry's Commentary.

[40] C.S. Lewis, cited in Josh McDowell, *Evidence that Demands a Verdict,* (Arrowhead Springs: Campus Crusade for Christ, 1972) 107-108.

[41] Donald G Bloesch, *Jesus Christ: Saviour and Lord* (Carlisle: Paternoster Press, 1997) 23.

[42] S.J. Samartha, *One Christ—Many Religions* (New York: Orbis Books, 2000) 106.

ABOUT THE AUTHOR

John Gillespie travels to pastors in the Majority ("Third") World. He is privileged to serve these modern-day heroes of the Faith, simple pastors, who live for Jesus and love His Church in poor and often persecuted lands.

John is married to Tessa, and they have been blessed with seven children, and countless "sons and daughters' in Christ. Together they love to cycle, walk, and pour themselves into the next generation of Jesus Followers.

John and Tessa Gillespie pastored churches in the UK for twenty-six years and in the USA for four years. They currently live in Overland Park, Kansas.

CPSIA information can be obtained
at www.ICGtesting.com
Printed in the USA
FFOW04n0724061014
7790FF